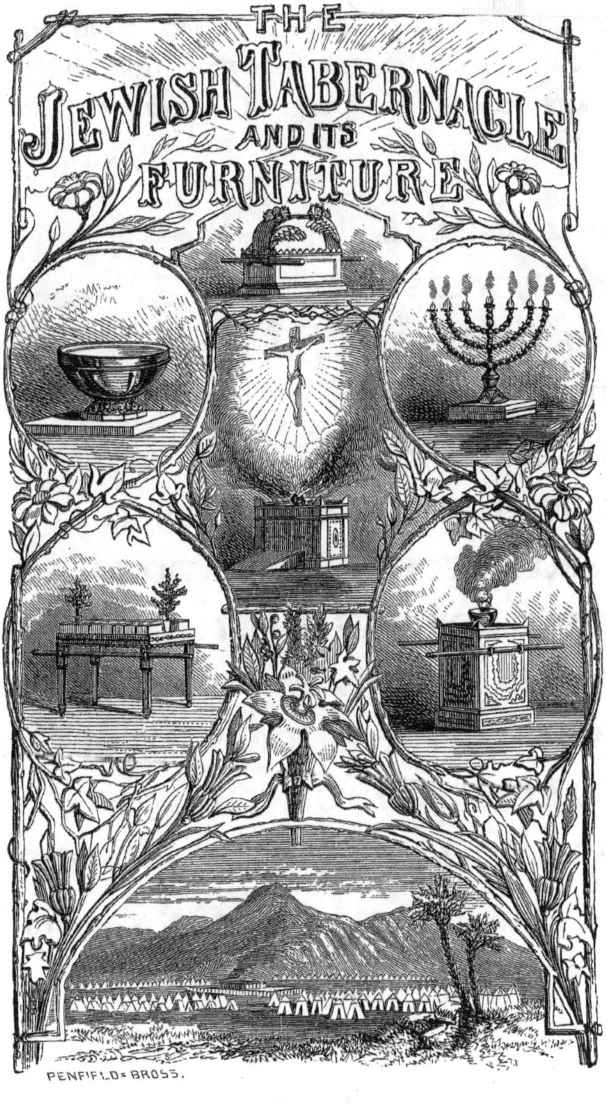

THE JEWISH TABERNACLE AND ITS FURNITURE

PENFIELD & BROSS.

OTHER RICHARD NEWTON TITLES

In addition to *The Jewish Tabernacle* Solid Ground is delighted to offer the following titles by the man nicknamed by CH Spurgeon *The Prince of Preachers to the Young.*

BIBLE ANIMALS

BIBLE JEWELS

BIBLE MODELS

BIBLE PROMISES

BIBLE WARNINGS

HEROES OF THE EARLY CHURCH

HEROES OF THE REFORMATION

THE LIFE OF JESUS CHRIST FOR THE YOUNG

THE KING'S HIGHWAY

RAYS FROM THE SUN OF RIGHTEOUSNESS

RILLS FROM THE FOUNTAIN OF LIFE

THE SAFE COMPASS AND HOW IT POINTS

Order these and more than 200 other titles at

solid-ground-books.com

sgcb@charter.net

1-866-789-7423

THE
JEWISH TABERNACLE
AND ITS FURNITURE,
IN THEIR TYPICAL TEACHINGS.

BY

REV. RICHARD NEWTON, D.D.,

RECTOR OF THE CHURCH OF THE EPIPHANY, PHILADELPHIA.

SOLID GROUND CHRISTIAN BOOKS
BIRMINGHAM, ALABAMA USA
205-443-0311

Solid Ground Christian Books
PO Box 660132
Vestavia Hills AL 35266
205-443-0311
sgcb@charter.net
solid-ground-books.com

The Jewish Tabernacle and its Furniture
by Richard Newton (1813 – 1887)

First Solid Ground Paperback Edition June 2009

Taken from the 1864 edition published by
Robert Carter & Brothers, New York, NY

Cover design by Borgo Design, Tuscaloosa, AL

ISBN: 978-159925-212-4

PREFACE.

When St. Paul desired to point out the relation existing between the Mosaic economy, with its rites and ceremonies, and that which has succeeded it, he compared the former to a *shadow*, and the latter to a body, or *substance*, by which that shadow was forecast. Colossians ii. 17. The relation existing between a shadow and the substance which projects it is easily understood. But all natural figures fail when applied to spiritual things. Ordinarily the shadow will afford nothing but the most general and unsatisfactory idea of the nature of the substance which projects it. And when that substance is reached we can gain no further knowledge respecting it from the shadow. But it is different in the case before us. The Jewish Tabernacle did more than this in preparing the way for the reception of the gospel. It gave very suggestive hints not only of the general outline of the glorious substance to which it stood related, but also of the particular blessings which were to be introduced by it. And even after this expected substance has been revealed, and with all its privileges in our possession, we cannot, without loss, wholly separate ourselves from the shadow of the preceding dispensation. It is, to us, a most significant and instructive shadow.

In no part of the New Testament is the glory of the gospel revealed in clearer, fuller light than in the Epistle to the Hebrews. And the light which shines so radiantly there is reflected from the Tabernacle and its services. That Tabernacle was designed of God not only to foreshadow the gospel before it came, but also to illustrate it after it had come. And as there is none "who teacheth like Him," so no illustration of the gospel and its blessings can be found comparable to that which is here furnished by Him. It is as a luminous illustration of the gospel that the Tabernacle is presented in this volume. The writer has found the attempt to unfold this illustration very precious and profitable to his own soul. His earnest prayer is, that every reader of these pages may be blessed with a similar experience. If God shall honor this unpretending volume by making it the means of leading one soul to the knowledge of Christ, or of giving to any who do know Him a clearer apprehension of the fulness and preciousness of His salvation, this will be regarded as an abundant recompense for the labor bestowed upon it.

In preparing these discourses much assistance was obtained from the valuable notes which accompany Bagster's large book of plates illustrative of the Tabernacle; from an admirable little volume entitled "Scripture Symbolism," by the Rev. Samuel Garrett, of London; and also from some very suggestive unpublished "Notes on the Tabernacle," prepared by Thomas Latimer, Esq., of this city, which were kindly loaned to me.

May He with whom the design of the Tabernacle originated, and who called Moses up the mount to study the pattern shown him there, crown with His rich blessing this humble effort to illustrate the truth of His gospel in the light which shines upon it from the Tabernacle, for Jesus' sake!

CONTENTS.

CHAPTER I.
THE NATURE AND DESIGN OF THE TABERNACLE......... 9

CHAPTER II.
THE BRAZEN ALTAR.................................. 51

CHAPTER III.
THE LAVER... 93

CHAPTER IV.
THE CANDLESTICK................................... 137

CHAPTER V.
THE TABLE OF SHEW BREAD........................... 183

CHAPTER VI.

THE ALTAR OF INCENSE 227

CHAPTER VII.

THE ARK 271

CHAPTER VIII.

THE CHERUBIM 315

CHAPTER IX.

THE MERCY-SEAT 359

CHAPTER I.

The Nature and Design of the Tabernacle.

"The First Tabernacle—was a figure for the time then present."—Hebrews, ix. 8, 9.

THE TABERNACLE AS PITCHED IN THE WILDERNESS
[FRONTISPIECE]

Jewish Tabernacle.

I.

Let us imagine ourselves, my friends, in the Desert of Sin, that gloomy, desolate region of country that lies between the north of Egypt and the south of Canaan. We take our stand near the foot of Mount Sinai. The time of our imaginary visit is, not the middle of this nineteenth century after Christ, but about the middle of the sixteenth century before Christ. We suppose ourselves to have travelled backwards on the stream of time, over the broad track of thirty-five centuries. It is the time of Israel's Exodus from Egypt. A nation of from three to five millions of people are marching through the wilderness under the visible, manifest guidance of the Lord Jehovah. Earth never witnessed such a procession before. No parallel to it has ever been seen since. The mysterious pillar of cloud, the august symbol of the divine presence, goes before them to lead them on their way. But now, they reach the foot of Sinai, and that cloud becomes stationary. The procession halts. In the beautiful order which God has indicated, the weary tribes now pitch their tents, to abide for a season round about that mountain, which was destined henceforth, in the most sacred sense, to become classic ground in the history of our race. On the summit of that mount God comes down in awful majesty. He spreads his pavilion there of clouds and darkness. The lightnings flash; the thunders roar; the mountain shakes, and the sound of the angel's trumpet waxes long and loud in attestation of the transcendent state of Heaven's great King. Moses is called up thither. With trembling awe he obeys the call. We watch him as he ascends the mount. Higher, and yet higher we see him rise. Now the clouds shut him in, and he is there, *alone with God*. He remains there forty days. There he receives the law, written by God's own finger, on tables of stone. And there, too, he is instructed as to the nature and design of that tabernacle and its furniture which he was commissioned to build. A diagram, a model, or type of it, formed by angelic, or divine hands, is set before him. He studies it out there, in all its detail, in the light of the upper sanctuary, and with God himself at hand as his teacher. And when he has learned his lesson well, he is sent down to execute the high commission entrusted to him, with this reiterated injunction:—

"See thou make all things according to the pattern showed thee in the mount."

No other structure was ever erected on our ruined earth, in the building of which God manifested such an interest, and in preparation for which, so much care and pains were lavished. But we know that God does nothing in vain. We know, too, that He never over-estimates the importance of any thing. His estimate of things is the true standard by which we are to form, and correct our own judgments. Surely then, when we see what an amount of care and time God was pleased to bestow on the preparation of the tabernacle and its furniture, we may well feel that the consideration of it should receive our most careful and attentive study. To such a study, my dear friends, I now invite you, with the humble prayer that God may bless our meditations.

Our theme will be, *The Jewish Tabernacle and its Furniture in their Typical Teachings.*

Our attention now, will be given to a general consideration of *the Tabernacle, in the Nature and Design of its Structure.*

I shall not attempt to enter into all the minute details of this sacred structure. This would not be either interesting, or instructive. Nor is it necessary. They are written out in the books of Moses. You can read them there for yourselves. Our desire now is to get a clear, and distinct general idea of the whole structure. Well, then, we imagine that Moses has descended from the mount, and fulfilled the important commission with which he was intrusted. He has finished the Tabernacle. Everything about it is completed. It is set up, with all its furniture, in the most exact conformity to the beautiful order of the pattern showed him in the mount. The tribes of Israel, in goodly array, are still encamped around it. Now, let us imagine ourselves to be a company of strangers, who have heard of the erection of this heaven-devised edifice, and have obtained permission to approach, and make a general survey of its wondrous parts. Our first view of the encampment bursts upon us as we gain the height of a commanding hill in the horizon. What a sight do we behold! A nation, of from three to five millions of people, is encamped in beautiful order before us! The camp is in the form of an oblong square. For miles and miles, as far as the eye can reach, it stretches out, in beautiful proportions. There, in the centre, we behold the wonderful tabernacle. Above it is suspended the pillar of cloud, the mysterious symbol of Jehovah's presence. The upper part of the cloud is seen to spread itself out, on every hand to the limits of the encampment, offering a grateful shade to protect the wanderers from the intensity of the sun's rays. As we stand and gaze upon the scene, we enter into the feelings of Balaam; when from the top of Mount Peor, he actually beheld the sight which we are imagining; and we feel constrained to take up his language and exclaim :— "How goodly are thy tents, O Jacob! and thy tabernacle, O Israel! As the valleys are they spread forth; as gardens by the river-side; as trees of lign-aloes which the Lord hath planted, and as cedar-trees beside the waters. He hath not beheld iniquity in Jacob, neither hath he seen perverseness in Israel: the Lord his God is with him, and the shout of a king is among them. God brought them out of Egypt; he hath as it were the strength of a unicorn. Surely there is no enchantment against Jacob, neither is there any divination against Israel: according to this time it shall be said of Jacob and Israel— What hath God wrought!"

But now let us descend from our distant and elevated point of view. Let us draw near, and make a closer examination of the interesting object before us. We are approaching the encampment from the East, coming upon it in what may properly be termed the vanguard of the mighty host. It is on this side that the entrance to the sacred enclosure lies, and *only* on this side that access to it can be had. And pursuing our way, in this direction, the first thing that we encounter, before we reach the camp, and quite outside of all its lines, is a fire, burning on the ground. It is the fire at which the sin-offering was consumed "*without the camp.*" Here, though just on the verge of the encampment, we must yet be at least four miles distant from the tabernacle. The three tribes of Judah, Issachar, and Zebulon are encamped here, in front of the tabernacle. They number together nearly two hundred thousand men, and none of their tents are allowed to be pitched nearer to the tabernacle than two thousand cubits, or three thousand five hundred feet, or about two-thirds of a mile.

This fire *without the camp,* in which the bodies of the animals presented as sin-offerings, on the great day of atonement, as well as on certain other occasions, were consumed to ashes, what solemn thoughts it suggests to us! How significantly it points us to Jesus! He was God's chosen Lamb, our great sin-offering. And "that He might sanctify the people with His own blood, he suffered *without the gate.*"

There, the devouring flame of the divine justice consumed this innocent sufferer, extorting from Him, in the hour of His final agony, the bitter cry:—"My God! my God! *why* hast *Thou* forsaken me?"

But we can not linger here. We pass through that portion of the camp which forms the van of the host. The tribe of Judah occupies the central position here. We make our way between the tents of Judah. Now, we reach their inner lines, the side of their encampment next to the tabernacle. Here, between these lines and the eastern, or front side of the tabernacle enclosure, there is left the space of two thousand cubits, already referred to. This broad space encircles the enclosure on every side. None of the camps are allowed to be pitched nearer the sacred structure than this. Midway in this space, and directly in front of the entrance to the enclosure are erected the tents of Moses and Aaron, and Aaron's sons. We pay our respects to the venerable legislator in passing, and proceed. But before entering this enclosure, let us take a walk round the outside of it, so as to form a correct idea of its external appearance. Turning to the right then, we soon reach the north side of the enclosure. Here, on our right hand, are encamped the tribes of Asher, Dan, and Naphtali. Their united camp numbers over one hundred and fifty thousand men. We proceed along the broad avenue which lies before us, and midway in this avenue, between the camp of Dan and the north side of the sacred enclosure, we meet the tents of the sons of Merari. They number over six thousand men, and as Israel pursue their journey, they have charge of the boards, and bars, and pillars, of which the tabernacle is composed. Proceeding on our way we now reach the west end of the tabernacle inclosure. Encamped on our right, we have the tribes of Benjamin, Ephraim, and Manasseh. They form the rearward portion of the host, in number about one hundred and eight thousand. Directly in front of them, and midway between their camp and the sacred court, are the tents of the sons of Gershon. They number seven thousand five hundred men, and have charge of the tent, the coverings, and the hangings connected with the tabernacle. Continuing our way along this broad, surrounding space, we now reach the south side of the sacred place. Here are encamped the tribes of Gad, Reuben, and Simeon. They number over one hundred and fifty thousand. In front of them, between their tents and the south wall of the central inclosure, we pass the tents of the sons of Kohath. They number eight thousand six hundred men, and have charge of the ark, the table, the candle-stick, the altars, and the vessels of the sanctuary. Passing on from thence, we soon return to the point from which we started, in front of the sacred inclosure. As we stand here this inclosure is before us. It is in the form of an oblong square. Its length, from east to west, is one hundred and seventy-five feet. Its breadth, from north to south, is eighty-seven and one-half feet, its height eight and one-half feet. It is formed by curtains of fine linen, suspended on pillars. These pillars are made of shittim, or acacia wood, overlaid with brass, and furnished, at the bottom, with fillets of silver made to fit into sockets of brass. When set up they are strengthened by stays, on each side, attached to stakes driven into the ground. There are twenty of these pillars along each side of the inclosure: ten at the end, and ten in front. Between these pillars are hung linen curtains, which form the walls of the inclosure. The space, thus inclosed, is called "The Court of the Tabernacle." The entrance to this hallowed place is called "The Gate of the Court." It is on the east of the court, and is formed by a beautifully embroidered curtain of blue, purple, and scarlet, suspended on four pillars. Its width is thirty-five feet. This is the only entrance. The material and color of this curtain are precisely the same as those of the vail, which hangs before the ark in the Holy Place. That vail, we know, on the best authority, typifies Christ. This curtain, then, which is like it, must be a type of Christ too. What striking significance this circumstance imparts to those passages of Scripture, in which Jesus said—"I am the door,—no man cometh unto the Father, but by me." It was a truth in the days of Moses, it is a truth now, and it will remain a truth forever, in the history of our ruined world, that there is no way of access to God, for life and light and salvation, but through Jesus Christ.

But now we pass through this gate, and find ourselves within "the Court of the Tabernacle." Here, the first object that meets the eye, is the altar of burnt-offering. A little beyond this stands the brazen laver. We pause not now to speak of these, as we shall return to them again, and dwell on them in detail. Passing by these, we proceed to the western end of the court. Here we come to the great central object of interest—the Tabernacle itself.* This is an oblong structure, forty-five feet in length, and fifteen feet in height and breadth. It ranges, in the direction

* See Frontispiece.

of its length from east to west, having its entrance, like the court which surrounds it, on the side which looks toward the east. The two sides and the west end constitute a frame work composed of boards of acacia wood overlaid with pure gold. There are twenty of these boards on each side, and eight at the west end. Each board is furnished with two tenons and sockets, and also with five rings or staples, through which bars are thrust for the purpose of bracing and steadying the whole structure. When thus erected, four separate curtains are spread over the tabernacle, to protect it and its furniture, from the changes of the weather. The first of these is of linen, with variegated colors of blue, purple, and scarlet. The second is a white curtain of pure, fine wool. The third is of goats' skins dyed red, and the fourth, a thick, heavy covering of badgers' skins.

This tabernacle is divided into two apartments of unequal size. We enter the first of these, which is the larger of the two. We are now in what is called the *Holy Place*. Above our heads is the first beautiful covering of which we have just spoken, embroidered with Cherubim in blue, purple, and scarlet. On either hand are the sides of the tabernacle glittering with gold. Everywhere are marks of sprinkled blood, the covenanting sign of peace. On the north, or the right hand, is the golden table with the twelve cakes of show-bread, *ever* before the Lord. On the south side, or the left hand, is the seven-branched golden candle-stick, *ever* lighted before the Lord; in the centre, before us, stands the golden altar *ever* fragrant with the morning and evening incense. Thus in God's house there is continually before Him *light*, and *fragrance*, and *food*. And there, beyond the golden altar, and shutting out the view of the Most Holy Place, hangs down before us the vail, the dark, mysterious vail. Beyond it, we know, is the ark of the covenant. But we may not draw that vail aside, or pass behind it, to gaze on what it hides from view. Only *one*, out of all the tribes of Israel, and he but once a year, may enter there, and behold the glory which fills that most sacred of all earthly spots.

Thus we have attempted to take a general survey of the structure of the tabernacle. Let us look now at its nature.

It was a *simple* structure. The materials of which it was composed were costly indeed. It is estimated that near a million of dollars were expended upon it. There was also much of artistic grace and beauty wrought up into its composition, and yet, compared with the splendid cathedrals of the old world, those gorgeous and gigantic masses of breathing marble, which men have erected, how simple and unpretending the tabernacle was! Considered as the dwelling-place of Him who has heaven for His throne, and the earth for His footstool; who has spread out the heavens as His curtain, and gemmed them with stars, the tabernacle was a *simple* structure.

It was a structure of *divine origin*. Sir Christopher Wren planned and built the Cathedral of St. Paul in London, as a monument of his own genius. Michael Angelo left the impress of his genius on the Cathedral of St. Peters at Rome. But the Jewish Tabernable was indebted for nothing to the force of Man's creative faculty. It was not an imitation of any other earthly structure. It had its origin in heaven. God—the Great Architect of the Universe—planned it. The design was His, both in the conception, and in the development of all its details. Moses had nothing to do but copy the model set before him, and carry it out, in all its minutiæ. No part, or portion of it was left for him to fill up. From the glorious cherubim overshadowing the mercy-seat, down to the cords and stakes which sustained the walls of the outer court, everything was to be made and fashioned "according to the pattern showed him in the Mount." *Such was the* NATURE *of this structure.*

It remains for us to consider ITS DESIGN; or the purpose of God's wisdom and goodness which it was intended to subserve. In handling this part of our subject, we must consider its design *in reference to the Jews,* and *in reference to ourselves.* To the Jews, the tabernacle, with its furniture and services, was at once *the source of present blessing*, and *the pledge or promise of future good*. It was a source or channel, through which the Jews in the wilderness were put in the possession and enjoyment of present, peculiar blessings.

"The camp of Israel was preëminently the place of blessing. It was the bright spot in the midst of a dark and desert world; for God was there, and walked in the midst of His people, to bless them, and deliver them from their enemies." Israel had no blessing which did not come to them through the tabernacle, or in connection with it. Their happiness, their comfort, their safety, their very existence depended on its instrumentality. Here was the Ark of God's presence, with the blood of the Lamb sprinkled upon it, ever speaking peace. Here was the burnt-offering on the brazen altar, the sweet savor from which, was ever rising before the Lord. Here was that gracious cloud which shaded them by day, lighted them by night, and was their guide in all their wanderings. The Psalmist tells us, cv. 39: "He spread a cloud to be a covering." From this it would seem that the majestic column, or pillar of cloud, which hung, suspended by divine power, over the tabernacle, spread itself out on every side to the utmost borders of their encampment, so as to screen the weary wanderers from the direct rays of the sun, and the reflection from the burning sands around them. There was no water in the wilderness, but the stream from the smitten rock followed them. The manna fell daily round about their tents. The feet of the wanderers were never swollen, and their garments waxed not old upon them for forty years. They were *the Lord's chosen family, at peace with Him through the blood of the everlasting covenant.* "The eternal God was their refuge, and underneath were the everlasting arms." Well might Moses, as he stood on the top of Pisgah, looking back on the one hand, at the way by which they had been led through the wilderness, and looking forward on the other hand, over all the glorious inheritance which lay before them, break forth in the rapturous exclamation:— "Happy art thou, O Israel; who is like unto thee, O people saved by the Lord, the shield of thy help, and who is the sword of thy excellency!" Thus the tabernacle was to Israel *a source of present blessing*.

It was at the same time, *a pledge or promise to them of future good*. It was a typical structure. St. Paul tells us in our text that—"The first tabernacle was a figure for the time then present." He speaks of it elsewhere, (Hebrews, x. 1.)

as "a *shadow* of good things to come." Now a *shadow* takes its general shape or form from that of the body or substance which projects it. You can form a tolerably correct idea of what that substance is when you see the shadow. But the tabernacle, with its furniture and services, was the shadow cast into the midst of the Jewish people by the plan of God's salvation in Christ, as it was eventually to be revealed. It was a heaven-devised symbol, prefiguring or typifying that salvation. To those among the Jews who understood its meaning it was a sort of illustrated profession of faith. It was their creed in symbol. To an intelligent, pious Jew, there must have been something very awe-inspiring, stirring, and suggestive in the solemn services of the tabernacle. We can imagine such a one standing by the altar, on which the victim he had brought was being offered. It is a shadowy service in which he is engaged, but he feels that it is very significant. With his bodily eye he surveys the shadow, but the eye of his soul is fixed with an intense gaze upon the future, searching after the substance by which that shadow is forecast. And as he does this, glorious glimpses of the "good things to come" are often disclosed to him. Suppose you are standing on an elevated summit which overlooks a broad, extensive landscape. The far-off parts of it are shrouded in gloom, and very indistinctly seen. But as you stand and gaze, there comes a burst of sunshine. It penetrates the most distant parts of the field of vision, and lights up the whole scene with a flood of glory. You see objects now which you had not perceived before; while others that were dimly seen, stand revealed in clear and vivid distinctness of outline.

The future, before the Jew, was such a landscape. His position of privilege connected with the worship of God set him on a lofty elevation, from which to look out upon the scene before him. As he looked abroad on the landscape, however, through the shadowy service of the dark dispensation with which he was connected, it was but a twilight view he obtained. The clouds and shades that rested on the landscape, made the circle of his vision very circumscribed. But sometimes a burst of sunshine, like that of which we have spoken, was vouchsafed the worshipper. Abraham was thus favored, when standing by his altar on Mount Moriah, "he desired to see Christ's day, and he saw it, and was glad." As the prophetic landscape of the future lay outstretched before him, it was lighted up with such a burst of spiritual sunshine. And doubtless such gleams of light were often granted to the believing Jews, as, in humble faith, they waited upon God in the service of the tabernacle. Every thing there seemed to have a finger with which to point to the Messiah, and a voice with which to tell of the gracious offices He was to fulfil. The cry of the innocent victim, the sight of his streaming blood and dying agonies, how powerfully these would speak of the dreadful nature of sin, and of the tremendous penalties which it incurred. The ascending flame from the altar of burnt-offering, with its curling smoke, and the fuming incense from the golden altar, would point to the atoning influences that were to go forth from the *coming lamb*, of which those then offered were but types. The candle-stick with its perpetual light,— and the table over-against it, with its unceasing furnishment of bread, would tell of divine illumination, and of grace in its abundant outflowings, sufficient for all the possible wants of the people of God. The unseen glories of the Most Holy Place, shut out from view by the mysterious vail, would whisper to the worshipper, of the bliss and brightness of that world, whose joys "eye hath not seen, nor ear heard, nor has the thought of them entered into the heart of man." And thus every part of this marvellous structure, with its array of imposing services, would seem to be inscribed all over, by the finger of prophecy, with intimations and promises of coming blessings, and as the humble worshipper gazed in faith upon them, the inspired tracery would seem to glow and sparkle in characters of heavenly light before him, weaving themselves out into glorious predictions of the untold things which "God hath prepared for them that love Him."

Thus the Tabernacle was to the Jews a *source of present blessing,* and *a pledge of future good.*

To us, the tabernacle is instructive as affording an *illustration of the blessings of the gospel;* and *a figurative view of our relation to the heavenly world.*

We see in it an *illustration of the blessings of the gospel.* The tabernacle was a sheltered inclosure in a dreary desert. In this respect, how truly it represents the Church of Jesus Christ, which is

> "A little spot inclosed by grace,
> Out of the world's wild wilderness."

In the tabernacle there was the typical lamb offered in daily sacrifice; in the gospel we have the true Lamb, which was once offered for the sins of the whole world, and which "perfects for ever them that are sanctified." In the tabernacle there was manna, by eating which the bodies of the people were preserved in life; but in the gospel we have the true Manna, the bread which came down from heaven, and of which whosoever eateth shall live forever. In the tabernacle and its service, they had water to drink that flowed from the smitten rock, "which Rock was Christ" in figure. In the gospel we have that Rock, not in figure, but in fact, opening up in the heart of each of His followers, "a well of water that springeth up into everlasting life." In the tabernacle was the golden candle-stick shedding its light continually on all that was in the Holy Place. In the gospel we have the Holy Ghost, "the Lord and Giver of Light," whose divine illumination pervades the minds of all His people, "making darkness light, and crooked things straight before them," and causing the truth to shine into their hearts, so that they "shall know all things." In the tabernacle they had the cleansing laver for purifying the bodies of the priests and Levites,—but in the gospel we have "the fountain opened for sin and for uncleanness," in which the vilest of the vile may plunge, and wash their guilt away. In the tabernacle was the golden altar with its ascending incense *typical* of the acceptance of the prayers and services of God's people; but in the gospel we have the golden altar of the Cross of Christ, with the incense of His great sacrifice ever rising before the throne of God, not *typifying*, but *insuring* the acceptance of His people's prayers and services. In the tabernacle was the pillar of cloud to lead onward the whole camp of Israel when they were to journey; but in the gospel we have the assurance of personal guidance through all the labyrinthian windings of life's intricate mazes. The promise to every believer runs—"I will guide thee with my counsel, and afterwards receive thee to glory." "Thou shalt hear a voice behind thee saying—this is the way walk thou in it, when thou turnest to the right hand, or when thou turnest to the left." The relation which God sustained, in this respect, to Israel as a nation, He now sustains to His people as individuals. He shades them by day, He enlightens them by night; He strengthens and comforts, He guides and blesses them as their own personal God. And thus, whatever blessing we see Israel enjoying in the tabernacle, in figure, we find believers now enjoying in Christ, in fact, and in fulness. And hence we see in the tabernacle an illustration of the blessings which we enjoy in the gospel.

But *further than this, the tabernacle fur-*

nishes us with a figurative view of our relation to the heavenly world.

St. Paul tells us distinctly that the tabernacle and its services were "patterns of things in the heavens." Hebrews, ix. 23. They were the counterpart of the very pattern which Moses himself saw in the mount, and in accordance with which he erected the whole structure. The wilderness in the midst of which the Tabernacle was set up, represented the world. The Court of the Tabernacle and the Holy Place represented the Church on Earth, in its different departments. The Most Holy Place represented the Church in Heaven. And as we gaze upon the intimate relation in which these two parts of the tabernacle stood to each other, the thought seems naturally to force itself upon us, how near we may be to that world which lies within the vail! We are often tempted to think and feel as if that world must be at an immense distance, a vast remove from us. A proper consideration of the tabernacle would seem to correct this impression. Look at it for a moment. Here you see the Holy Place, or the Church on Earth, and the Most Holy Place, or the Church in Heaven, in the closest possible contiguity to each other. There is only that thin material vail to separate them. We know that "angels and ministers of grace" attend us continually. We know that—

"Millions of spiritual beings walk our earth,
  Unseen, both when we sleep and when we wake."

We cannot tell how near to us, how closely about us are the things of the unseen world. If the mantle of invisibility were but removed, we should see things "in heaven and earth that we have scarcely dreamed of in our philosophy."

"Surely, yon heaven, where angels see God's face
   Is not so distant as we deem
From this low earth? 'Tis but a little space,
   The narrow crossing of a slender stream;
'Tis but a vail which winds might blow aside;
Yes, these are all that us of earth divide
From the bright dwelling of the glorified,—
   The Land of which we dream!

Those peaks are nearer heaven than earth below,
   Those hills are higher than they seem;
'Tis not the clouds they touch, nor the soft brow,
   Of the o'erbending azure, as we deem.
'Tis the blue floor of heaven that they upbear;
And, like some old and wildly rugged stair,
They lift us to the Land where all is fair,—
   The Land of which we dream."

Or in the language of another poet—

"From this world to the next
How short and peaceful may the passage be!
One beating pulse, one feeble struggle o'er,
May open wide the everlasting door.
Yes! for that bliss, unspeakable, unseen,
Is ready—and the vail of flesh between,
   A gentle sigh may rend."

Is it possible that we may be thus near

the awful realities of the eternal world? O surely, then, it becomes us to—

> "Walk thoughtfully on the solemn shore
> Of that vast ocean we must sail so soon!"

And thus we see how the tabernacle is instructive to us *as affording an illustration of the blessings of the gospel; and a figurative view of our relation to the heavenly world.*

In conclusion the subject we have now considered suggests to us—*How thankful we should be for the day in which we live!*

It is "the day of salvation." It is the dispensation of the substance which succeeded to that of the shadow. It is the time of direct and full revelation as opposed to the time of type and figure. It is to the dispensation of the tabernacle what the hour of noon, with its radiant splendor, is to the hour of early dawn, with its dim twilight and its gloom. It was the deep sense He had of the superior glory and privilege of this period of the Church's history which led our Saviour to say to His disciples:—"Blessed are your eyes, for they see, and your ears, for they hear. For verily, I say unto you, that many prophets and righteous men have desired to see the things which ye see, and have not seen them; and to hear the things which ye hear, and have not heard them." In regard to light, and grace, and privilege, our position under the gospel is exalted indeed. And if it be true that "to whom much is given, of them much will be required," then it becomes us to see well to it, that we improve diligently our privileges. It is a sad, sad thing, when we see men exalted to heaven by the abundance of the blessings showered upon them, only that like Capernaum of old, they should, in the end, be thrust down to hell. Let not this melancholy doom be ours, my Christian friends! O, let us look at the full-orbed circle of our blessings, and see what love,— what gratitude—what zeal—what devotion should be ours! Let us seek the grace which will enable us to walk worthy of our high calling, and to render to the Lord according to all His unspeakable goodness to us. Constrained "by the mercies of God, let us present ourselves a living sacrifice, holy and acceptable to God, which is our reasonable service."

And, my dear friends, who are not Christians, if connection with the covenant of God's grace in Jesus is so blessed, how can you be satisfied to remain without a personal interest therein? You are still wanderers in the gloomy wilderness of this fallen world. The dangers and discomforts, and deprivations of the wilderness are all yours. You have no covenant cloud to shelter and guide you. No sacrifice puts forth its atoning efficacy in your behalf. There is no living water from the Smitten Rock, of which you can drink to satisfy the longings of your thirsty soul. There is no bread from heaven, of which you can eat to sustain and strengthen your famishing spirit. Unsheltered, weary wanderers in this waste howling wilderness, I take my stand to-night by the gate of entrance to the gospel tabernacle, and in the name of its Builder Jesus, I invite you to come in. Here is the sheltering, guiding cloud; come, rest beneath its shadow. Here is the Heavenly Lamb whose blood alone has power to cleanse from all sin, come and let Him sprinkle your guilty soul with His precious blood. Here is the water of life flowing clear as crystal. It will follow you all through the wilderness. O drink, and your soul will be revived, and you will live. Here is the bread that cometh down from heaven. Come, eat of it, and your soul will never hunger again. Here is light that streams down from the golden candlestick of the upper sanctuary. Its revelations are wonderful. Come and see what they are. Here is the incense of unceasing intercession—come and share in its untold benefits. It is Jesus bids you come. "The Spirit and the Bride say, come. Let him that heareth say, come. Let him that is athirst come : and whosoever will, let him come, and take of the water of life freely." There yet is room---come !

CHAPTER II.

The Brazen Altar.

"The fire shall ever be burning upon the Altar; it shall never go out."—LEVITICUS, vi. 13.

THE ALTAR OF BURNT OFFERING.

Jewish Tabernacle

II.

In a volume of published sermons of the eloquent Henry Melvill there is an interesting discourse on Christ's victory over Satan. It is founded on the words—"For this purpose was the Son of God manifested, that He might destroy the works of the devil." In proceeding to speak of the history and character of Satan, he says:—"How abruptly is the tempter introduced upon the scene! There is no account given of this mysterious being; but suddenly, without the least intimation who the invader is, or what region he had heretofore traversed, a fierce irruption is made into the youthful paradise, and creatures formed in the very image of God, dislocate their own happiness, and that of a countless posterity. There seems to be a chapter wanting, and the history of the *defeat of man* appears to demand a history of the *conqueror* of man. We should be better prepared to account for evil gaining a footing on earth, if we were furnished with an account of its first appearance in the universe. But this is wanting."

We cannot but experience a feeling akin to this, when we come to consider the subject of burnt-offerings, or animal sacrifices in connection with the worship of God. The first notice that we have of these very significant and suggestive acts of divine worship, takes us back to the very gates of Paradise. There we see Abel, standing beside his altar, and the smoke of the flame which consumes the innocent victim, is ascending to heaven in our sight. We see the offering of sacrifices introduced by men, as a part of the worship of Jehovah. We see it accepted of God, and continued, from age to age, through a period of four thousand years, till Christ came, (God's own provided, spotless Lamb,) to take away the sins of the world. And yet, the strange thing about it is, that there is not a single word, recorded or revealed, about the *origin* and *institution* of sacrifices. Here again there seems to be "*a chapter wanting.*" We see a most solemn and important rite of divine worship in established use, without having any account whatever of its introduction. And yet there is not the least shadow of doubt as to the authority by which it was introduced. The idea of taking away the life of innocent creatures, in typical atonement for man's sin, could never have originated in the mind of man. And it never could have been accepted of

God, or continued in connection with the worship which His people offer to Him, if it had been a mere human invention. This argument is conclusive. If we could put our finger on the chapter and verse, in the early part of Genesis, which contained the account of the inauguration of these sacrifices, we should not feel a whit more certified, that they had their origin in the authority and command of God.

This train of introductory thought was suggested by the consideration of the Brazen Altar, or the altar of burnt-offering, which is to be the theme of our present meditation.

There were two altars connected with the Jewish Tabernacle. One of these was a large altar, the other was a small one : one was made of brass, the other was made of gold ; one was designed for the offering of burnt-sacrifices, the other for the offering of

THE BRAZEN ALTAR. 57

incense; one stood without, in the Court of the Tabernacle, the other stood within the Tabernacle, in the Holy Place itself. It is the *first* of these that we are now to consider. The other will come up for our consideration hereafter.

This first altar was distinguished from the other in two ways. It was denominated, by way of excellence, "*The Altar*." Our English word altar is a very unmeaning one. The etymology of it has no significance at all. It comes from the Latin word *altus*, and that denotes nothing but a high, or elevated place. The Hebrew word for altar is one which conveys the idea of a sacrifice. It comes from an old root which signifies to slay, or to slaughter. So that when the Hebrew spoke of the altar, the very term which he employed told him of a place, where sacrifices were offered, where blood was shed, and life was taken away.

The other phrase, used to designate this piece of the furniture of the tabernacle, was "the altar of burnt-offering." The Hebrew word for burnt-offering denotes that which *ascends,* or mounts up, as the flame and smoke did on this altar, when the victim was consumed upon it. That which was presented on this brazen altar, was a whole burnt-offering. Every thing connected with it ascended, or went up to God. And contemplated from this point of view, what a beautiful type this altar of burnt-offering was of the cross, our altar, our *only* altar in the Christian Church, and on which Jesus, the heavenly Lamb, was offered. He was emphatically a *whole* burnt-offering. It is said of Him that "He gave *Himself* for us." Yes, His *entire* self. He kept nothing back. Body, soul, and spirit; his entire

THE BRAZEN ALTAR. 59

humanity, his absolute divinity, went to make up the sacrifice. Hence we read in one place, that "God spared not His *own Son*, but delivered Him up for us all." And hence also we read in another place of "the Church of *God*, which He has purchased with *His own blood*." All, therefore, that went to make up the person of God's own Son in the complex nature of His mysterious being, we are to regard as constituting the *whole burnt-offering*, which Jesus presented, for us, on the cross.

We notice next the *materials*, of which this altar was composed. These were two, viz., shittim, or acacia wood, and brass, which overlaid and covered the wood in every part. There was a need for the employment of both these materials. The wood, if not protected by the overlaying brass, would have been consumed by the flame, which burnt up the offering, while the brass, if employed alone in the construction of the altar, would have made it too heavy for the purposes of transportation in their journeyings through the wilderness.

Now this altar of burnt-sacrifice, with the offerings presented upon it, stands before us as a type of Christ and his cross. And the materials, of which the altar was composed, point strikingly to His two-fold nature. His humanity, if found alone, would have been consumed by the fire of divine justice, which blazed forth against Him, when He stood as our substitute, and bore our sins, in His own body, on the tree. And then, on the other hand, His divinity, if found alone, like the altar, if all of brass, would have been too oppressive for us. It would have made us afraid by its excellency, and would have overwhelmed us by its majesty. But blended with the

THE BRAZEN ALTAR. 61

humanity, and tempered and softened by its transmission through the vail of flesh, it meets our necessities in every respect, and furnishes us with just the help and comfort that we need.

In its *form and dimensions* the altar of burnt-offering was a square, hollow box, without either top or bottom. It was five cubits broad, and three cubits high. Reckoning the cubit at eighteen inches, this would give us seven feet six inches for its breadth, *i. e.*, for the length of each of its sides, and four feet six inches for its height. It was just twice the size of the ark, and was the largest article of furniture connected with the tabernacle. There were four horns, or projections, one on each corner of the altar. These may have been in part for beauty, and in part also for use. It is to these that the Psalmist refers when he speaks of "binding the sacrifice with cords, even unto the horns of the altar." There was a grating of brass, which stretched across the whole interior of the altar. It was not level with the top of the altar, but was placed some distance below the top. On this grating the sacred fire was kept ever burning. In the language of the text it was "never to go out." There were different brazen vessels also connected with the service of this altar. There were shovels for gathering up the ashes, and pans, in which they were carried away, and basins for receiving the blood, and flesh-hooks for handling the pieces, and fire-pans, in which the sacred fire was carried and kept alive as they went onwards in their journeyings.

The one *use* to which this altar was devoted, was that of consuming the yearly, the weekly, and the daily sacrifice. Here the lambs were continually slain and offered unto God. And from this hallowed spot, from the blood here shed, from the fire ever-burning here, and the victim consumed therein, there went forth unceasingly those atoning influences, which in a ceremonial, or figurative sense, purged the consciences of the worshippers from sin, and rendered their persons and services acceptable to God. And now, having dwelt thus far on the structure and use of the altar of burnt-offering, we are prepared to consider the lessons we may gather from it, when regard is had to its typical teachings.

In proceeding to this part of our subject, there are five different points of view, from which we may contemplate this altar, each of which will furnish us with a distinct lesson of great practical importance.

And the first thing to which I would call your attention in connection with the altar of burnt-offering is the PROMINENCE *assigned to it in connection with the Jewish Tabernacle.*

Just look at its position. It stood immediately in front of the gate of the tabernacle, or the entrance to the sacred enclosure. It was the first object which met the eye of the worshipper, as he drew nigh to present his offering to God, and the last which he beheld on retiring from that service. Its place was the outer court. It was not hidden in some deep recess, some inner shrine, removed from the gaze of sinners; nor did it stand within the tabernacle to be sought for by many, but to be reached and seen only by a few. No; but it was placed in the sight of all. Some parts of the tabernacle furniture were hidden from the public view. The candlestick, the table of shew-bread, and the golden altar of incense were within the Holy Place, which none but the priests

THE BRAZEN ALTAR. 65

might enter. And the ark of the covenant was behind the vail, in the Most Holy Place, where only the high-priest might enter on the solemn day of annual atonement. But it was very different with this altar. It was not hidden. There was no screen before it. "Nothing surrounded it but a thin fence of fine-twined linen, or net-work, which concealed nothing, and within which the whole congregation might pass at their pleasure. It was plainly visible from without. It invited attention, and no one could help seeing it without wilfully, turning away his eyes. From day to day the smoke went up, and the blood streamed down from it, a pledge that all who would, might be purged from pollution there."*

We have no material altar. The Lord's table, which some ignorantly, and others

* Garrett's Scripture Symbolism.

presumptuously designate an altar, is not an altar, and should never be called by that name. The Christian Church never has had any altars, and, without making void the gospel, it never can have. "When Popery overran the Church with its errors, altars were introduced. But when the Reformation dawned, they were removed. There was nothing, indeed, about which the Reformers were more careful, than the purging of the Churches from these relics of superstition. The Romish altars were taken down, because they were symbolical of error, just as the brazen altar was built up, because it was symbolical of truth. And our Reformers excluded the word altar from the Prayer Book, as carefully as the altar itself from the Church." *

But though we have no material altar, we have that which the brazen altar dimly

* Garrett's Scripture Symbolism.

shadowed forth. The cross of Christ, on which he was once offered, "the just for the unjust, to bring us to God;" *this* is our altar. Not the *wood* of the cross, but the *sufferings* of the cross, the one perfect atonement, once made there "for the sins of the whole world."

Look now at the position which God assigned to the altar of sacrifice in the Jewish Tabernacle, that heaven-sketched symbol of the Church. Behold one of the marks of a true Church. It will give great prominence to the altar, the cross of Christ, or the doctrine of His atoning sacrifice. "Let us imagine ourselves at the door of a Romish church. It is broad day-light; but as we look through a small open door into the church, all is dark. Scarcely anything is visible. Presently, far off in the distance, in a gloomy recess, a mysterious sort of shrine, it is just possible to discover the form of an altar, with two lighted candles on it. Everything is contrived with admirable scenic effect, to give that impression of awe, concealment, and mystery, which is so characteristic of the worship of that Church. What a contrast you have here between the enshrined altar of Popery, with its deep recesses, its covering screen, and its 'dim religious light,' on the one hand, and God's altar on the other, in the open court of the tabernacle, in the full light of day, and before the eyes of all men!"*

The Tractarian writers in our own Church have taught what is known as "*the doctrine of reserve.*" They would have the atonement of Christ and the great truths centring in it, kept in the background, and not made prominent in the ordinary ministrations of the sanctuary. But you cannot look upon

* Garrett's Scripture Symbolism.

the Court of the Tabernacle, and see where God placed the altar of burnt-offering, without feeling how solemnly He rebukes such an idea as utterly erroneous. The altar of the Christian Church, like that of the Church in the wilderness, must always take precedence. It must stand in the forefront of everything. The office of the Christian Church, and the Christian Ministry is, not to hide away the altar in dark recesses, and behind overshadowing screens; not to hold back the doctrine of the atoning sacrifice of Christ, and keep it in reserve, but to set it forth in the broad light of day;— to hold it up before the eyes of all men;— to proclaim it from the house-tops; to preach it "first, last, midst, and without end;" to "know nothing else among men save Jesus Christ, and him crucified." This lesson we are taught when we see the *prominence* assigned to the altar of burnt-offering in the tabernacle.

In taking our second look at this altar, we notice THE RELATION WHICH IT BORE TO EVERY OTHER PART OF THE TABERNACLE. It was the most important part of the whole tabernacle. Like the root to the tree, like the foundation to the building, like the fountain to the stream, like the mainspring to the watch, like the heart to the body, it was that, on which every other part of the sacred structure depended, and from which it derived all its value. The tabernacle itself could not be entered, nor any part of its hallowed furniture be made use of, till it had been sprinkled with the blood of the victim offered upon this altar. Take away the altar of burnt-sacrifice, and every part of the tabernacle, however splendid, would have been useless. Beyond it stood the laver, in which the priest might desire to wash. In the tabernacle stood the golden candle-stick, shedding around its hallowed light; over against it was the table of shew-bread, ever furnished with its abundant supply of food; and between them, just before the vail, stood the golden altar, from which the fragrance of sweet incense went up continually. Yet there was no way of access to any of these but by the brazen altar. *That* must be first approached. And not only did the way of access to them lie *by* this altar, but it was *from* it they derived all their efficacy. They were formed of shittim wood, and overlaid with gold, and wrought into forms of exquisite beauty; but they could not begin to subserve the different offices, for which they were designed, or be of the slightest use to the worshippers, till the blood shed upon the brazen altar had been sprinkled upon them. This must be first applied to everything. The priests, their garments, the sacred vessels, the ark itself, all were unfit for service, were worthless for the purposes of worship, till the blood from the altar had touched, and sanctified them. How instructive! How suggestive! This altar represents the cross of Christ. As we look at it from this point of view, we seem to see written on it as with a sunbeam, the great practical truth, that the way to heaven,—the *only* way by which any of our ruined race can enter there,—*lies over Calvary*. There is no pardon, no renewal, no acceptance, no righteousness, no peace, no grace, no blessing, no salvation to any of Adam's children, but through the sacrifice once offered upon the cross. What an illustrated commentary, this brazen, blazing altar affords, of the truth and meaning of the apostle's words, when he declares that "without the *shedding* of blood there is no remission." Yes, but then it is equally a truth, that without the *application* of that blood there is no remission. It is not the blood as *shed* that sanctifies and saves, but the blood as *applied*, or *sprinkled*.

And this is true not of our *persons* only, but of our *services* also. No function of the officiating priest could be discharged, no act of worship on the part of the waiting people could be accepted, till there had first been the intervention of the blood from the brazen altar. And it is precisely so with that, which this significant shadow typified. "Accepted *in* the beloved," is the great underlying doctrine of the gospel. Our prayers, our praises, our sighs, our tears, our repentance, our faith, our words, our actions, our labors, our sufferings, our vows, our alms-givings, our sermons, our sacraments,—all things that may be crowded into the entire circle of our services,—have worth, or merit, not in themselves, but only as they stand connected with the sacrifice which Jesus offered on the cross, and are sprinkled with His atoning blood, in all its prevailing efficacy. This lesson is taught us by the relation, which the brazen altar bore to every other part of the tabernacle.

Our third lesson from this altar is suggested by the CONTINUITY *of the offerings presented upon it.*

There was to be no cessation, no suspension, or interruption of the service here rendered. The command of God was imperative on this point. The law of the offering was most stringent in this respect. The words of our text contain God's law respecting it:—" The fire upon the altar shall be burning in it; it shall not be put out; and the priest shall burn wood upon it every morning, and lay the burnt-offering in order upon it. *The fire shall ever be burning upon the altar; it shall never go out.*" Here you see the *continuity* of these offerings especially provided for. Morning by morning, evening by evening, week by week, month by month, and year by year, they were to be kept up. The necessity for applying to this altar would be a constantly recurring one. There was no hour in any day, or any night, when some transgressor would not require to avail himself of the benefits of the offering here presented, and hence the sacrificial flame was never to go out. But here the Jewish type, or shadow, fails of accurately representing the Christian antitype, or substance. The continuance of the sacrifice on the brazen altar of the Jewish Church could only be maintained by the *repetition* of the offering. But there is a continuance of the sacrifice in the Christian Church, though the offering once made on our altar, the cross, has never been repeated. And the explanation of the difference is very simple, and as satisfactory as it is simple. The sacrifice on the Jewish altar was an *imperfect* sacrifice, and hence the necessity for its repetition. They were "sacrifices," as St. Paul says, "offered year by year continually, which could never make the comers thereunto perfect." Our sacrifice, offered upon the cross, is a perfect sacrifice, and therefore it needs no repetition. It was offered "once for all;" and by this one offering, Jesus, our great High-Priest, "perfects forever them that are sanctified;" *i. e.*, all His believing people. The offering was once made, but the merits, the influence, the efficacy of the offering, abide continually. And because it thus abides, there needs no repetition of it. A repeated sacrifice is imperfect, and good for nothing. And if the sacrament of the Lord's supper is a real sacrifice, a repeated sacrifice, as the Church of Rome, and Romanizing teachers in our own Church affirm, then we are no better off than the Jews were. Our sacrifice is as imperfect as theirs was. The repetition of it would prove it so. But it has never been repeated. Yet it is a *continual* sacrifice. Come to it in youth, or in age, by day or by night; come to it twenty times a day; come as often as the consciousness of sin recurs to you, and you will find it always the same. On our altar of the cross "the fire is ever burning; it never goes out." The fulness of its efficacy never abates in the slightest degree. The hand of faith stretched out to it, the eye of faith directed towards it, will never fail to secure the benefit of its power to atone, to pardon, to bless, to save. It is a precious lesson, which the continuity of the offerings on the altar teaches.

Our fourth lesson is taught us, when we consider the EFFICACY OF THE OFFERINGS *presented on the brazen altar.*

You may say, indeed, that we have just spoken of their *imperfection*, and that is true. So far as "purging the conscience from dead works" was concerned; as to the actual "taking away of sin," or as the apostle expresses it, as to "making the comers thereunto perfect," the Jewish sacrifices were inefficacious. But, remember that *this* is not what they were designed for. And it is always proper to take into consideration the design had in view in the ordaining of any law, or the establishment of any service, before you affirm inefficacy, or failure, as characterizing it. John the Baptist was sent, not as the Messiah, but as one whose office was to bear witness of Him. If John were judged by the standard of our expectations in regard to Christ, we

THE BRAZEN ALTAR. 79

should say he was a failure. But judge him by the light of what he was sent to do, by the witness he bore to Christ, and you see that John was no failure. He was an efficient, faithful witness-bearer.

The morning-star is not the sun. It is only sent to herald the sun's approach. Weigh the morning-star in the sun's balances, and it will be found wanting. You will pronounce it an imperfection, a failure. But consider what its mission is, the Creator's design respecting it, to act as the fore-runner of the king of day, and you will see only the perfection of beauty in the mild radiance of its silver rays.

And just so it was with the sacrifices offered on the brazen altar. They were not intended to do for the Jews what the sacrifice of Christ does for us. They were only types, or shadows of that sacrifice. Of course they could only have a typical, or shadowy efficacy. *This*, however, they had in perfection. They were only designed to impart a ceremonial cleanness. They were only intended to qualify the comers thereunto to engage acceptably in the worship of God, and through faith to seek from Him the benefits and blessings of that great sacrifice, which they represented, and which was, in the fulness of time, to be offered. Their office was very limited, or circumscribed. But so far as this office, or design, extended, they were *perfectly efficacious*. And here the brazen altar points significantly to the cross of Christ. It speaks to us, in eloquent tones, of the thorough efficacy, the absolute perfection of the sacrifice He offered. The Jewish altar, with its sacrifice, did perfectly what it was designed to do. And so it is with the Christian altar, the cross, and the sacrifice there offered. It was designed to put away sin, and it does this so perfectly, that God says of those who are interested in this sacrifice, that their "sins are blotted out as a cloud;" they are "cast into the depths of the sea;"—they "shall not be remembered, nor come into mind." The sacrifice of the cross was designed to secure pardon to penitent believers, and it does this so perfectly, that God declares of those who trust in it, that he "does not behold iniquity, nor see perverseness in them." The sacrifice of the cross was designed "to bring in everlasting righteousness," and it does this so perfectly, that those who are arrayed in the robes of salvation, which Jesus puts upon His people, are declared "*faultless*," not when judged by erring human standards, but when the decision comes from the unerring standard of the court of heaven. "Without spot or wrinkle, or any such thing," is the verdict uttered concerning them. They stand before God on the same level on which His own beloved Son stands. He proclaims to all the Universe, that "they are righteous *even as He is righteous.*" This is glorious. How perfect that sacrifice must be, from which results *so* perfect as these flow out to a ruined world! Perfect pardon, perfect righteousness, perfect peace, and perfect salvation, these are the blessed fruits which flow out, to us, from the sacrifice of Christ. And they are fruits which may be gathered now. They may be gathered all along the pathway of our pilgrimage, as the returning penitent stretches forth the hand of trembling faith, and lays hold upon the altar. The efficacy of Christ's sacrifice is taught us as we gaze upon the brazen altar from the point of view now before us.

The fifth and last lesson taught us by this altar is seen, when we observe the EXTENT OF ITS BENEFITS.

It was open to all. Not only might all of the Jewish nation draw nigh to this altar, and share in its blessings, but all of any other nation might do the same, if they would come in the way which God pointed out. There were restrictions and limitations about the Holy Place, and the Most Holy Place, but there were none about the brazen altar. Only the priests could enter within the vail, and have access to the mercy-seat, but the people—*all the people*—might have access to the altar of burnt-offering. The vilest of the vile, all, who would, might come, and avail themselves of its benefits. We have seen that it was perfectly effectual to accomplish all the objects, for which it was designed. The point before us *now*, shows us that, so far as regards its merit, or worthiness, or power to bless, the sacrifice of the brazen altar was an unlimited sacrifice. All Israel did not seek, or secure an interest in the benefits of the sacrifice offered upon this altar; but the altar was there for all, and the benefits emanating from it were there in abundance sufficient to meet the necessities of all. This point I hold to be perfectly clear. No one can pretend to call it in question. And when we proceed to argue from the type to the antitype, from the shadow to the substance, in reference to a point as clear and cardinal as this, the argument is one of great power. There is no such thing as fairly resisting it. It amounts to a sort of practical demonstration. The ceremonial atonement made by the offerings presented on the brazen altar of the Jewish Tabernacle was not a limited atonement. Neither was the atonement, by the sacrifice of Christ upon the cross, a limited atonement. The brazen altar of the tabernacle forbids our entertaining such an idea. The doctrine of a limited atonement is plainly contrary to the teachings of "the pattern shewed to Moses in the mount."

Of course, if you watch the progress of the gospel in our world, you will see directly, that all men, to whom the gospel is preached, do not receive it, or yield their hearts to its influence. Unless then you take in the idea of universal salvation, you must admit that there is a limit in reference to the atonement, somewhere or other. This limit can only refer to one of two things; there must be a limit, either in the application of the atonement, or in its original merits. But then there is the widest possible difference between these two things. I believe most firmly in a limited atonement, so far as the *application* of its benefits, to the individuals of our race is concerned. In other words, I believe that a portion of our race, and not the whole of it, will be saved by the atoning sacrifice of Christ. I believe, moreover, that this limitation is controlled by the absolute sovereignty of God. The doctrine of election, as taught in Scripture, and embodied in the seventeenth Article of our Church, is the proper point of view, from which to contemplate this matter of the limitation of the atonement, in its practical application to the souls of men.

But, so far as the worth or merit of Christ's atonement is concerned, I believe it to be utterly and absolutely an unlimited atonement. Unless I believed this, with my whole heart, I could not be a preacher of the gospel. If I believed that Christ died for a portion of our race only, and not for the whole, how could I, as an honest man, stand up in a promiscuous assembly like this, and exhort all who hear me, to draw nigh to the altar of Christ's cross, and seek the application to their souls of the saving benefits of His sacrifice? If I believed that the atonement was limited in this sense, how could I expound Hebrews, ii. 9, which speaks of Christ as " by the grace of God *tasting death* for *every* man?" How could I work up into such a system of theology that stubborn passage in 1 John, ii. 2, in which the apostle affirms that Christ is " the propitiation for our sins, and not for ours only, but also for the sins of the *whole world?*" If these passages do not teach an atonement absolutely *un*limited, as to its merits, how is it possible for such a truth to be taught? If I believed the atonement limited, as to its merits, by anything less than the necessities of our whole race, I could not officiate as a minister in the Episcopal Church; for here, on every communion occasion, I am required to stand by the sacramental table, and in the most solemn part of that most solemn service, to affirm of the atonement of our blessed Lord, that it was "a sacrifice, oblation, and satisfaction, *full, perfect,* and *sufficient for the sins of the whole world.*" If I believed the atonement of Christ limited, in its merits, I had rather go to the stake, and give this body to the flames, than be guilty of the solemn mockery of making such a declaration. But the teachings of the gospel, and of our Church, on this subject, harmonize entirely with the foreshadowings of the brazen altar, and agree with "the pattern showed to Moses on the Mount." They lead us to think of the merits of Christ's sacrifice as adequate to the necessities of every ruined child of Adam's guilty race.

And thus, from *the prominence assigned the brazen altar;*—from *the relation it bore to every other part of the tabernacle;*—from *the continuity of its offerings;*—from *the effi-*

THE BRAZEN ALTAR. 89

cacy of its sacrifices; and from *the extent of its benefits,* we gather up the several important, practical lessons, taught us by this part of the tabernacle furniture.

In conclusion, I would waive all other reflections suggested by this subject, to dwell for a moment on this one thought; viz., *how absolutely unspeakable are our obligations to God for the sacrifice of His Son!* This is the one fruitful source of all our blessings. Stand up in the centre of the circle which surrounds you, as God's creature, and tell me what single thing there is, on which you can lay your finger and say, "here is one thing, at least, which I could have possessed and enjoyed, if Christ had never hung upon the cross." From the least to the greatest there is no such thing. You have no *temporal* blessing, which the sacrifice of Christ did not purchase for you. Your life, your health, your strength, the use of your faculties, your home, your relatives, your friends, the bread you eat, the water you drink, the raiment you put on, the air you breathe, the sunshine which gladdens you, everything in the catalogue of your temporal blessings, you owe to the sacrifice once offered upon the cross. And the same is true of all our spiritual mercies. These sabbaths, these sanctuaries, these sacraments and sermons, this precious volume of God's written word;—the privilege of prayer, the power to pray,—pardon, peace, light, grace,—all that sustains for the present, and all that cheers and encourages for the future,—the blessed hope of eternal life, a title clear to an inheritance of unfading bliss, all, all is due to the sacrifice offered on the altar of the cross. Connection with this sacrifice brings us into the charmed circle of the covenant of salvation. It exalts us to the highest point of possible distinction. All that the human mind, in its wildest revellings, has ever imagined, in the way of marvellous changes and wondrous exaltations, bears no comparison with the change wrought in the position and prospects of a ruined sinner, and the affluence of blessing secured to him, by a saving personal connection with the sacrifice of Christ. The simple truth here is stronger than any fiction ever coined by poet's fancy. The romance of history in real life is sometimes strange, but the romance of revelation is infinitely stranger. We have this romance, in its marvellous result, epitomized, in a single verse, by the Psalmist, when speaking of God's dealings with his people in the gospel of his Son, he says that "He raiseth up the poor out of the dust, and lifteth the needy from the dunghill; That He may set him with princes, even with the princes of his people." This is the transformation wrought by a saving connection with the sacrifice of Himself, which Jesus offered on the cross. Well might the apostle resolve to glory only in that cross! Beloved hearer! are you personally interested in that cross and its sacrifice? If so, rejoice, and be exceeding glad. Make full proof of the benefits of that sacrifice, and let your life show how unspeakably it blesses you.

If you have no such interest in the cross, resolve, by the help of God, without delay to seek it!

CHAPTER III.

The Laver.

"And the Lord spake unto Moses, saying, Thou shalt also make a Laver of brass, and his foot also of brass, to wash withal; and thou shalt put it between the Tabernacle of the Congregation and the Altar, and thou shalt put Water therein."—EXODUS, xxx. 17, 18.

THE LAVER.

Jewish Tabernacle.

III.

In our last discourse, the brazen altar was the theme of our meditation. That was a part of the furniture of the Tabernacle, with which the element of fire was connected. On the altar the flame was burning continually. The brazen Laver is to engage our attention on the present occasion. This was a part of the furniture of the Tabernacle, with which the element of water was connected. " Of all inorganic substances," says a distinguished writer, " water is the most wonderful. We can think of it as the source of all the changefulness and beauty, that appear in the clouds; then as the instrument by which the earth was modelled into symmetry, and its crags chiselled into grace; then, as in the form of snow, it robes the mountains it has made, as with a mantle of transcendent light, which we could not have conceived, if we had not seen; then as it exists in the foam of the torrent,—in the iris which spans it, in the morning mist which rises from it, in the deep crystalline pools which mirror its overhanging shore, in the broad lake and glancing river;—and finally in that, which is to all human minds the best emblem of unwearied, unconquerable power, the wild, various, fantastic, tameless unity of the sea. And as we thus think of it, we are constrained to ask, what shall we compare to this mighty, this universal element for glory and for beauty?" We find an answer to this inquiry in the subject which now comes before us.

"Thou shalt make a laver of brass,"

said the Lord to Moses, "and thou shalt put *water* therein." Here we find this element of beauty, this mighty, resistless, all-pervading, universal agency of nature pressed into the service of religion, and made to minister at once both to the worship and honor of God, and to the spiritual welfare and happiness of man.

The laver, like the altar of sacrifice, was symbolical in its character. The great lesson taught by the part it bore in the worship of the tabernacle was the importance of purity on the part of all who drew nigh to God, the absolute necessity of thorough sanctification for the polluted, through the operation of the Spirit and truth of God. *How* this great, practical lesson was taught by the laver and its watery contents, we shall see as we proceed with the subject.

It is worthy of notice that the laver was the only article of furniture connected with the Jewish Tabernacle, of which we have no account furnished, either as to its form, or its dimensions. This is certainly very singular, when we bear in mind the extreme care and precision, with which these specifications are given, in reference to every other part of the sacred structure. No reason is assigned for this omission, and it is vain to speculate on the subject.

The *form* of the laver is generally supposed to have been circular. This is the most natural form, in which to make an article of this kind. And we know that that, which Solomon subsequently made for the use of the temple, was circular, and doubtless he would be guided in this matter by a desire to imitate, as far as possible, what Moses had made "according to the pattern showed him in the mount."

In addition to the laver itself, the text informs us that Moses was commanded to make "his foot also of brass to wash withal." The word here rendered "foot" has occasioned much perplexity to commentators. "Our impression is," says Dr. Kitto, "that the laver, whatever were its shape, stood upon another basin, more wide and shallow, as a cup on a saucer; and that the latter received from spouts, or faucets in the upper basin, the water which was allowed to escape, when the priests washed themselves with the water, which fell from the upper basin. If by the under basin we understand the 'foot,' spoken of in the text, the sense is clear. The text does not say that the priests were to wash themselves *in* the basin, but *at* it. *In* it they could not well wash their hands and feet, if the laver was of any height." The Jewish Rabbins say the laver had several faucets, or "nipples," as they call them, from which the water was let out as wanted. *How* the priests washed their hands and feet at the laver seems uncertain. That they did not wash *in,* either the laver, or its base, seems clear, because then the water, in which they washed, would have been rendered impure by those who washed before, or with them. The Orientals, we know, dislike exceedingly, to wash in a basin after our manner, in which the water, with which we commence washing is clearer than that with which we finish. They always prefer to wash at a falling stream, where each successive affusion is of clean water. We incline therefore to think, that the priests either washed themselves with the stream, as it fell from the spouts into the base, or else received in proper vessels so much water as was needed for the occasion. The Orientals, in their washings, make use of a vessel with a long spout, and wash at the stream which issues thence, the waste water being received in a basin which is placed underneath. This seems, to us, to illustrate the idea of the laver with its base, or foot, as well as the way in which the priests performed their ablutions. The laver had thus its upper basin, from which the water fell, and "the under basin for receiving the waste water."

The *material* of which the laver was composed was brass. In Exodus xxxviii. 8, we read, " And he made the laver of brass, and the foot of it of brass, of the looking-glasses of the women assembling, which assembled at the door of the tabernacle of the congregation." The word in the original, should have been rendered here *mirrors*, instead of looking-*glasses*. Glass mirrors were not known till the thirteenth century *after* Christ, while the tabernacle was built in the fifteenth century *before* Christ. The mirrors then in use were *molten* mirrors, made out of brass or copper, and highly polished. And those here spoken of were of this character. "We may understand," says the author of the Notes of the Pictorial Bible, "either that the stock of copper in the camp of Israel was so comparatively small, as to have been exhausted in the other works for the tabernacle; or else, that the material employed for the mirrors used by the women was of a superior quality, and for *this* reason it may have been made use of in the preparation of the laver. There is still another reason that has been assigned in explanation of this circumstance. As the women who assembled at the tabernacle are especially mentioned, it is not improbable that they followed the example of the Egyptian women, who took their mirrors with them when they went to the temple. Moses may have required the giving up of their mirrors to be employed in the preparation of the laver, in order to put a stop to a practice of which he did not approve."

I would venture to suggest another reason why the material of the mirrors was employed in the making of the laver. May it not have been with a view of illustrating its design? It was intended for the cleansing and purifying of the officiating priests. The material of which it was composed would admit of a fine polish. The whole exterior of it would thus constitute as it were one mirror. As the priests approached it, they would thus be aided in discovering the spots, and marks upon their persons, which were to be removed before they entered the sanctuary.

This laver was symbolical of the truth of God. This is compared to a mirror, which at once shows us our deformity, and aids us in the removal of it. Hence, says the apostle, speaking of the word of God, "We all, with open face, beholding as in a glass, the glory of the Lord, are changed into the same image, from glory to glory, even as by the Spirit of the Lord."

Let this suffice concerning the form and structure of the laver. We proceed now to consider the lessons which it teaches us, when considered in its typical character.

There are three principal points with which the lessons taught us by the laver may be connected. *In the first place, let us consider what we are taught by the laver with its supply of cleansing water.*

The purpose intended to be subserved by the laver was very different from that secured by the altar of burnt sacrifice. *That* had to do with the putting away of sin itself, while *this* had to do with the removal of the pollution resulting from sin. The former of these operations denotes, in New Testament language, the great work of justifying the

THE LAVER. 105

soul of the believer; the latter denotes the equally great work of sanctifying the soul. The brazen altar stands before us as the symbol, or representative, of justification: the laver stands before us as the symbol, or representative, of sanctification. And very suggestive these two symbols are of the different agencies by which the two great works referred to are effected. The altar with its innocent victim, consumed in the ascending flame, points to Jesus, the Lamb of God, dying for our sins, and rising again for our justification. The laver, with its abundant supply of pure cleansing water, points to the Spirit of God, and the truth through which that Spirit acts, as the great appointed instruments for carrying on the work of sanctification in the souls of believers. The water in the laver was an emblem of the Holy Spirit in His purifying work. And water is a scriptural emblem of the Spirit.

Our blessed Lord Himself taught us this. We read, you remember, in John vii. 38, that "In the last day, that great day of the feast, Jesus stood and cried, If any man thirst, let him come to me and drink. He that believeth on me, as the scripture hath said, out of his belly shall flow rivers of living water. But this," adds the evangelist, "spake He of the Spirit which they that believe on Him should receive." We have therefore the very clearest authority for considering water as an emblem of the Spirit. And how beautiful an emblem of the Spirit of God it is! *Water is pure.* Though not really so, it seems to be the simplest of all substances. It reflects the sunbeam from its glassy surface, or transmits it through its substance in almost equal brightness, giving us the idea of transparent purity.

And just such is the Spirit. He, too is pure, or rather purity itself. He is the great original fountain of all purity. Perfectly transparent the blessed Spirit is. He reflects and transmits, in all its brightness, the glory of Christ. This is His peculiar office. He reveals Jesus. "He shall take of mine," said Jesus, "and show it unto you." He testifies, not of Himself, but of Christ. The figure fails in this, that the water has no light in itself. It *transmits* it indeed, but does not originate it. With the Spirit it is different. He *imparts*, as well as transmits it. Spiritual light originates with Him. He is the Lord and Giver of it.

Again, *water is free.* It readily adapts itself to every possible variety of shape or form, as the jagged rocky border of the river or lake will show, but it cannot be restrained or bound by any. At one time, under winter's chilling touch, it is solid. Again, as in the laver before us, it assumes a liquid form;

and then again, beneath the heat of the summer's sun, it flies off in vapor, and becomes invisible. It is capable of gliding into a thousand forms of beautiful variety. And how apt an emblem of the Spirit we have here! Who can restrain or bind Him in His operations? "Where the Spirit of the Lord is, there is liberty." Like the wind, "He bloweth where He listeth, and thou hearest the sound thereof, but canst not tell whence He cometh or whither He goeth." As to Elijah on Horeb's awful top, He may reveal Himself now in the lightning's flash—again in the whirlwind's roar—then in the earthquake's crash—and yet again in the still small voice.

Water is pervading. The oceans, seas, lakes, rivers, and streams of earth are made up of it. But it is not confined to these localities. It pervades all nature. It is in the air we breathe, and the food we eat. It

THE LAVER. 109

is in the solid rock, and in the yielding clay. It is in the tree, the shrub, the flower, the grass. It is in the blood that courses through the veins of your body, and in the bones and marrow by which those bodies are upheld and nourished. It is a *universal* element. And so is the Spirit. Well might the Psalmist ask, "Whither shall I flee from thy Spirit?" Heaven, earth, hell, the mighty universe is filled by this Spirit! "The Spirit searcheth all things." Penetrating all hearts, and reading all thoughts and purposes; there is nothing hid from His presence.

Water is mighty in its operation. It is an element of prodigious power. Enclose it in a ball of iron, no matter how thick; let it freeze, and it will burst that iron. Shut it up in the centre of a mountain of solid granite, and in passing from the liquid to the solid state, it will upheave that ponderous mass and make an outlet for itself. And surely in its *power* this element fitly emblemizes the Spirit, who in His operation softens the hardest heart—subdues the most stubborn will, and upturns the very foundation of the kingdom of darkness.

And then water is a vitalizing element. All animal and vegetable life is dependent on its influence. Take it away from nature, and the gloomy pall of desolation and death would come down upon every thing. And so, in the spiritual world, it is with the Holy Ghost. Life never begins or continues without His influence. " He is the great moving power in the world of spirits, who alone is able to beat down the proud sufficiency of man's mind, or to raise it from the depths of wickedness and despair. He only can break in pieces the hard heart, or regulate the stormy will, or rouse the sleeping conscience, or curb the passion-tossed soul. He is the one life-giver, without whose quickening touch every soul of man must remain for ever in the gloomy charnel-house of spiritual death, a withered and desolate thing." Thus the laver with its water is an emblem of the Spirit.

It is also an emblem of the truth by which the Spirit operates. In quickening men into spiritual life, God's truth is the grand instrumentality employed by the Holy Ghost. Hence, says St. James, " Of His own will begat He us by *the word of truth*." Jesus compared this truth to water when He said to Nicodemus—" Except a man be born of water and of the Spirit, he can not enter into the kingdom of God."

And in the great work of cleansing, or purifying the souls of his people, the truth revealed in Scripture is, again, the instrumentality employed. Hence, when St. Paul speaks of Christ as cleansing or sanctifying

His church, he tells us it is done "with the washing of water *by the word*."—Ephesians v. 25. This means that just as the hands and feet of the priests, officiating in the tabernacle, were cleansed by the "washing of water" in the laver; so the souls of Christ's people are cleansed or purified by the word, as by the washing of water. And when we hear God saying by the prophet Ezekiel (xxxvi. 25), "I will sprinkle clean water upon you, and ye shall be clean: from all your filthiness, and from all your idols, will I cleanse you"—and compare this with the words of Jesus, in which He prayed for His people, saying, "Sanctify them by thy truth"—we see clearly that it is not the water of baptism which is referred to in these passages, but the revealed truth of God, which, in its quickening and purifying properties, is compared to water.

And thus the laver, with its abundant

THE LAVER. 113

supply of clean water, by which the priests were purified and rendered fit to enter the tabernacle, was an emblem of God's Spirit and God's truth, by whose quickening influence dead souls were made alive; and by whose cleansing power they were sanctified and made fit for the service of God.

This is the lesson we are taught by the laver with its supply of cleansing water.

But, secondly, let us inquire what lessons we are taught by the persons who used the laver.

It was *only the priests* who had access to the laver. It was not intended for all the people. The sacrifice on the brazen altar was for the whole assembly of the congregation—but not so the water in the laver. This was restricted to the use of those who were about to enter the sanctuary of the Most High, and engage in its hallowed exercises. There are three important practical lessons taught us by this part of our subject. *We see here the true character of God's people; the high privilege accorded them; and the nature of the service required of them.*

We are taught here *the true character of God's people.* Those who washed in the water of the laver were *priests.* But this laver with its cleansing water symbolized the Spirit and the truth of God in all their sanctifying influences as connected with the Christian Church. But in this Church God's Spirit is given, and God's truth revealed to every true member of the same. They all have access to this spiritual laver for the cleansing of their souls. But does the analogy fail, you are ready to ask, between the Jewish and the Christian laver as regards the character of those who have access to it? Not at all. How so, you ask again, when *only priests* were allowed to wash in the Jewish laver? The analogy holds strictly true, in this respect, for in the Christian Church *all the Lord's people are priests*. The apostle Peter has made this point perfectly clear. In his general epistle, addressed to all Christians, he says: "Ye also, as lively stones, are built up, a spiritual house, an holy priesthood, to offer up spiritual sacrifices, acceptable to God through Jesus Christ." 1 Peter ii. 5. Again he says, "Ye are a chosen generation, a royal priesthood." If you find any difficulty in adapting this language to the condition of God's people in the present life, bear in mind that it is now rather the language of prophecy or promise, than of actual present realization. *Priestly* functions, as well as kingly, are those which the redeemed are to exercise in the glorious future that awaits them. In the ascription of praise which St. John renders to Christ at the opening of the Apocalypse, he says, "Unto Him that loved us, and washed us from our sins in his own blood, and hath made us kings and priests unto God and his Father, to Him be glory and dominion for ever and ever." Rev. i. 5, 6. Soon after this the glorious vision of the heavenly world is unfolded to the beloved disciple. The panorama of its magnificence is spread out before him. He sees the white-robed company, with palms of victory in their hands, and crowns of glory on their heads, as they stand before the everlasting throne. He listens to the new song which they sing, the anthem of consummated redemption; and this is the chorus in which all voices join, as they fall down and worship the Lamb that sitteth upon the throne: —" Thou art worthy :—for Thou wast slain, and hast redeemed us by Thy blood, out of every kindred, and tongue, and people, and nation; and hast made us unto our God kings and *priests!*" Yes, priests, in the perfection of their sacred functions; this is the high character which the redeemed will bear in eternity.

And priests, in preparation for that elevated position, is the true character of the redeemed in time. The Christian Church, now on earth, is one vast theological seminary. Every member of that church is a student of divinity, a candidate for the ministry, a priest in training for the high office awaiting him in the glory of the heavenly state. This view of the character of God's people is taught us when we see the *priests*, of the Jewish dispensation, washing in the water of the laver.

We also learn here the high privilege accorded to them. One part of this privilege was to be pure. They washed continually and were cleansed. No ceremonial imperfection, or pollution clung to them. The water in the laver removed all such imperfection from them. Now this was a real privilege, even in the low typical sense in which they realized it. But what a shadow that privilege was compared with what God's people now enjoy in the "laver of regeneration;—the washing of water by the word" and Spirit, to which they have access continually! There the heart's deep stains, the spots upon the soul, are taken away. "Like a refiner's fire, and like fuller's soap," is the description God, Himself, has given of this marvellous provision of His grace for the cleansing of His chosen ones. And as they come to this spiritual laver day by day, the promise is fulfilled, and " He purifies the sons of Jacob as gold and silver is purified, that they may offer unto the Lord an offering in righteousness." And sanctified thus, by His word and Spirit, His people are " preserved blameless unto the day of His appearing." And as this washing is con-

THE LAVER. 119

tinued, the result will be that, finally, all the redeemed, " sanctified wholly in body, soul, and spirit," and made complete in holiness, will be presented before the throne of the Father " without spot or wrinkle or any such thing."

> " Their souls from sin for ever free
> Will mourn its power no more;
> But clothed in spotless purity,
> Redeeming love adore."

This is the high privilege accorded to believers in Jesus. And this privilege is beautifully fore-shadowed as we see the priests of Aaron's line made pure by the water of the laver.

The other part of the privilege, of these purified priests, was that they had access to the Tabernacle, the sanctuary where God dwelt.

The golden candlestick, always shining there, shed its hallowed light for them. The table with its show-bread offered its unfailing provision to them. And the golden altar with its fuming incense diffused its acceptable fragrance in their behalf. And, O, what significant types and figures, we have here, of the nobler privileges of that priestly people whom God hath pardoned through the sacrifice of His Son, and sanctified by the influence of His truth and Spirit! To them the way of access into the Holy Place—the place of God's immediate presence—lies open at all times. To them divine illumination is vouchsafed. "The manifestation of the Spirit is given to each of them to profit withal." "They have an unction from the Holy One, and know all things." They eat of the bread which cometh down from heaven, and never hunger. "They are abundantly satisfied with the plenteousness of God's house." Their prayers and praises, their persons and services, are always accepted of God, because they are presented continually before Him perfumed with the fragrant incense of the merits of Christ's most perfect sacrifice. And thus, as we behold the purified priests enter the sanctuary, we see beautifully typified the high privilege accorded to the people of God.

But we also see here illustrated the nature of the service required of them.

The washing in the laver was a thing requiring to be continually repeated. It was not an annual, or a monthly, a weekly, or a daily service, but one of unceasing recurrence. If the priest had occasion to enter the sanctuary twenty times a day, then twenty times a day he must wash in the laver. He could never enter without washing. What a practical, illuminated commentary we here have as to the meaning of the passage in which God said to the priests of that dispensation, " Be ye clean who bear the vessels of the Lord!" It was this which led the Psalmist to exclaim, "I will wash my hands in innocency, O Lord: *so* will I go to thine altar." And the great truth which is thus taught us, respecting the service required of those whom these priests represent, *i. e.*, the people of God under the present dispensation, is, that it should be characterized by thorough sanctification, by the most absolute and entire consecration of heart and soul. Hence, they are spoken of in one place as "a holy nation—a peculiar people—zealous of good works." Again, they are called "living sacrifices." They are "not their own—but bought with a price," and "constrained by the love of Christ to glorify God with their bodies and their spirits, which are His." Paul had risen, fully, up to the lofty standard of requirement here erected when he could say—"for me to live is Christ." And all that was typified in this respect by those unceasing washings at the laver, has been most sweetly expressed by one who has thus written:—

"Precious Saviour, may I live— Only for Thee.
Spend the powers Thou dost give— Only for Thee.
Be my Spirit's deep desire— Only for Thee.
May my intellect aspire— Only for Thee.
In my joys may I rejoice— Only for Thee.
In my choòsings make my choice— Only for Thee.
Meekly may I suffer grief— Only for Thee
Gratefully accept relief— Only for Thee.
Be my smile, and be my tears— Only for Thee.
Be my young and riper years— Only for Thee.
Be my singing and my sighing— Only for Thee.
Be my sickness and my dying— Only for Thee.
Be my rising and my glory— Only for Thee.
Be my whole eternity— Only for Thee."

And thus, *the true character of God's people—the high privilege accorded them—and the nature of the service required of them*, are the lessons we are taught by considering *the persons who used the laver*.

But there is a third and last point of view from which to contemplate this laver, and gather instruction from it, and that is THE POSITION IT OCCUPIED.

This is very significant. The direction given to Moses, on this point, was most explicit: "Thou shalt put it between the tent of the congregation and the altar." "The tent of the congregation" means the tabernacle. Thus the laver stood, by divine direction, midway between the brazen altar and the tabernacle. Now the instruction we gather from this part of our subject will depend on the view we take of what was symbolised, or represented by the laver.

Some maintain that the laver, in the Jewish Church, was a type or symbol of baptism, in the Christian Church. This opinion is held by those who incline to take what are known as High-Church views of the sacraments. But those who take this view will find the laver, thus considered, a very unmanageable piece of the tabernacle furniture. It cannot be made to harmonize with what is known as the High-Church system. In this system, when fairly represented, the baptismal font is made to stand at the porch, or vestibule of the Church. It is regarded as the initiatory rite of the Church, or the door of entrance to it. It is the first thing with which one, desiring to enter the Church, has to do. But this, you perceive, is to invert the order established by God in the Jewish Church. The Jew was required to come first to the brazen altar, with its propitiatory sacrifice, and then to the laver, with its cleansing water. But the Christian, who takes the view of which we are speaking, changes entirely this heaven-appointed order. He insists on coming to the laver for its cleansing first, and then to the altar for the benefit of its sacrifice. That this is not the view taken by the Episcopal Church is clear from the tenor of her baptismal services. In these, before she allows an adult person to be baptized, she requires, from him, a profession of repentance for sin, and faith in the Lord Jesus Christ. This is, in effect, to take him to the brazen altar first, and then to admit him to the laver with its washings.

And even the service for the baptism of infants is based upon the same principle. The parents or sponsors, coming with the child, are required to promise repentance and faith in the name of the child. Thus the child is considered as repenting and believing, hypothetically; and the blessings consequent upon the exercise of those graces, are promised hypothetically. That service, throughout, is framed on this hypothesis. So that if the laver be regarded as representing baptism, our Church in this part of her hallowed services does no violence to "the pattern showed to Moses on the mount." She does not set the laver on the other side of the altar, from that on which God set it. But, in the case of adult persons *actually*, and in the case of infants hypothetically, she requires first, an approach to the altar with its atoning sacrifice, and then she admits of access to the laver with its purifying water.

But we do not regard the laver as denoting baptism. It was, as we have seen, the type, or representation of the regenerating and sanctifying influences of the Spirit and truth of God, as experienced by His believing people. And, looked at, from this point of view the practical teaching of our subject is most interesting and important. It establishes for us, beyond all question, the great truth that regeneration does not precede, but follows pardon. The divine order, or arrangement in this matter is not regeneration first, and then pardon; but pardon first, and then regeneration. Not the washing first, and then forgiveness, but forgiveness first, and then the washing. Not the laver first, and then the altar, but the altar first, and then the laver. The brazen altar stands free to all. Nothing is necessary for one who would approach it but a sense of sin. We are not required to make ourselves clean in order that we may come to Christ—but we are to come to Him in order to be made clean. The tendency of our nature is to invert this order. In dealing with inquiring souls there is no difficulty you will encounter more frequently than that which developes itself in the saying: "I am not fit to come to Christ." This language is suggested by a desire to do something ourselves in order to remove our sin and pollution before coming to Christ. It is the struggling endeavor to get at the laver first, and then to approach the altar. "The altar stands nearer to the sinner than the laver. The Spirit leads him, with his heart unrenewed, to the cross of Christ. There he receives forgiveness. There he is clothed in the spotless righteousness of Christ. And then, but not till then, the Spirit sprinkles him with the water of regeneration. So writes St. Paul,—"Ye are all the children of God *through faith in Christ Jesus.*" And so St. John declares,— "*As many as received Him to them* gave He power to become the sons of God." Renewal cannot go before forgiveness. It must *follow* after it. When the sinner bathes his soul in the blood of Jesus, it is no matter of uncertainty whether or not it will be washed in the laver of the Spirit. It is as sure as that God is holy, as sure as that God is true, for heaven is the believer's by promise, and nothing unclean can enter there." Christ is made of God unto his people, first *righteousness*, and then sanctification. " Say not," observes good Archbishop Leighton, " Unless I find some measure of sanctification, what right have I to apply Him as my righteousness? This inverts the order, and disappoints thee of both. Thou must first, without finding, yea or seeking anything in thyself but misery and guiltiness, lay hold on Him as thy righteousness; or else thou shalt never find Him thy sanctification. Simply as a guilty sinner thou must flee to Him for shelter; and then, being come in, thou shalt be furnished out of his fulness, with grace for grace."

And thus we have seen what we are taught *by the laver with its supply of cleansing water;—by the persons who used the laver;—and by the position which the laver occupied.*

In conclusion, the thought which the consideration of this subject impresses on our minds with greatest force, is that of—*the infinite holiness of God.*

This truth flashes out before us from the flame which was ever burning on the sacred altar. We see it in the charred remains of the victim consumed there, and in the clouds of wreathing smoke that ascend from the altar. But we see the same truth in the laver also. It sparkles forth from every ray of light reflected from the surface of its crystal water. The liquid sounds of the splashing streams as they fall from the laver to the base are eloquent proclaimers of it. And we see it illustrated, O how impressively, in the unceasing washings performed there by the priests! "A little imperceptible dust, unavoidably contracted in their pathway through the wilderness, was sufficient to render them unfit for God's service. Even *this* would have exposed them to His consuming judgments, if they had attempted to minister before Him without its having been previously washed away. "When they go into the tabernacle, they shall wash with water *that they die not;* or, when they come near to the altar to minister, they shall wash their hands and their feet *that they die not.*" It was not only that gross defilements would unfit them for their ministry, and call down vengeance on their heads, but the slightest contact with uncleanness—a speck upon the hand or foot, rendered them obnoxious to the fire of judgment, if they ventured unwashed into the presence of that God "who looketh upon the heavens and they are unclean, and chargeth His angels with folly." How awful the majesty of this holy God! He dwelleth in the high and holy place. His name is holy. His nature is holy. "Without holiness no man can see the Lord."

> "Ah, how can guilty man
>   Be just with *such* a God?
> Who, who can meet Him and escape
>   But through the Saviour's blood?"

There is nothing that proclaims the necessity of the atonement more convincingly than this view of the infinite holiness of God. Stand by the laver with its cleansing water, and you are in the best possible position to understand the meaning, and feel the power of the truth embodied in the lines of the hymn which declares:

> "There *must* a Mediator plead,
>   Who God and man may both embrace,
> With God for man to intercede,
>   And offer man the purchased grace.
>
> And lo! the Son of God is slain,
>   To be this Mediator crown'd:
> In Him my soul, be cleansed from stain,
>   In Him thy righteousness be found."

How solemnly this subject speaks to you, my dear hearers, who are neglecting the process of cleansing which God has provided, and trusting to anything else to fit you for appearing before Him. No other washing would have sufficed for the Jewish priests save that which was conducted at the vessel appointed by God to hold purifying waters. If they had thought to cleanse themselves at some other washing place, of their own construction, instead of at the laver, they would have exposed themselves to the wrath of God, as much as if they had altogether neglected His commands. He had provided a process of cleansing, arranged according to His own will, and which He knew would fit them perfectly for His service. If they had sought another, it would have proved that they either despised His commands, or undervalued what He had furnished for their use. In either case they would have been guilty of a direct insult to the majesty, holiness, and wisdom of God. And what was true of the sign, is true of the thing signified. What was true of the shadow is much more true of the substance.

God has lifted up his son Jesus on the cross. In His blood, there shed, He has opened a fountain of cleansing. His great command to all the guilty and polluted children of men is: "Go wash in that fountain and be clean." Believe on the Lord Jesus Christ, and thou shalt be saved.

Have you washed in that fountain? If you have,—your sins are forgiven. Your soul is cleansed. Your salvation is secured. If you have not—your pollution clings to you still. "The wrath of God abideth on you." "If *I* wash thee not"—says Jesus to you, as He said to Peter—"If I wash thee not, thou hast no part in me!" No part in my pardon. No part in my righteousness. No part in my peace. No part in my salvation. O wash in this fountain and be clean!

> "The dying thief rejoiced to see
>   This fountain in his day;
> And there may we, though vile as he
>   Wash all our guilt away."

CHAPTER IV.

The Candlestick.

"And thou shalt make the seben lamps; and they shall light the lamps thereof that they may gibe light ober against it."—Exodus, xxv. 37.

THE GOLDEN CANDLESTICK.

Jewish Tabernacle.

IV.

The brazen altar enlisted the element of fire in its service. The brazen laver in its use employed the element of water. But the golden candlestick, which we are next to consider, connected with the part it bore in the solemn worship of the sanctuary the interesting element of *light*. Of all the elements of nature light is the most subtle, the most mysterious, and yet the most beautiful.

> "Prime cheerer, Light!
> Of all material beings the first and best!
> Efflux divine! Nature's resplendent robe!
> Without whose vesting beauty, all were wrapt
> In unessential gloom!"

Nothing can be a more appropriate handmaid of religion in her hallowed services than this interesting element. How beautifully the sweet-spirited Bonar discourses of its properties!

> "The light is ever silent;
> It sparkles on morn's million gems of dew,
> It flings itself into the shower of noon,
> It weaves its gold into the cloud of sunset,—
> Yet not a sound is heard; it dashes full
> On yon broad rock, yet not an echo answers;
> It lights in myriad drops upon the flower,
> Yet not a blossom stirs; it does not move
> The slightest film of floating gossamer,
> Which the faint touch of insect's wing would shiver.
>
> The light is ever pure;
> No art of man can rob it of its beauty,
> Nor stain its unpolluted heavenliness.
> It is the fairest, purest thing in nature,
> Fit type of that fair heaven where all is pure,
> And into which no evil thing can enter,
> Where darkness comes not, where no shadow falls,
> Where night and sin can have no dwelling-place!

We are all familiar with the use of this term light in Scripture, as expressive of

THE CANDLESTICK. 141

the character of God, and connected with His service. Hence we read that "God *is* light, and in Him is no darkness at all." It is said of Him that "He *dwelleth* in light." "He decketh Himself with light as with a garment." Jesus said of Himself, "I am the light of the world." And of his people it is said that they are "the children of light." We cannot wonder then to find the golden candlestick, and its heaven-derived light occupying a prominent place in the service of the Jewish Tabernacle.

Thus far, in our meditations on this subject, we have been standing in the Court of the Tabernacle, outside of the sacred structure itself. We now draw near, and enter the Tabernacle. Look for a moment at its form, size, and structure, before we enter.

It was an edifice of an oblong, rectangular

form. Its length was forty-five feet; its breadth and height each fifteen feet. The two sides and the western end were formed of boards of shittim wood, overlaid with thin plates of gold, and fixed in solid sockets, or vases of silver. Above they were secured by bars of the same wood, overlaid with gold, passing through rings of gold which were fixed in the boards. On the east end, which was the entrance, there were no boards, but five pillars of shittim wood, which, with their chapiters and fillets were overlaid with gold. These pillars were furnished with hooks of gold, from which hung a vail or curtain, of variegated colors. This curtain formed the door of the Holy Place. This entire enclosure was divided into two parts, by a vail or curtain which hung between them. The exact dimensions of these different parts of the tabernacle are not given us in the

THE HOLY PLACE, WITH THE VEIL OF SEPARATION.
Jewish Tabernacle.

THE HOLY PLACE, AND THE MOST HOLY PLACE.
(The Veil of Separation withdrawn.)
Jewish Tabernacle.

Scriptures. It is generally supposed, however, that it was divided in the same proportion as the temple, afterwards built according to its model. If this supposition is correct then, two-thirds of the whole length were allotted to the first room, or the Holy Place, and one third, to the second, or the Most Holy Place. Thus the Holy Place would be thirty feet long, fifteen wide, and fifteen high; and the inner appartment, or the Most Holy Place, would be fifteen feet each way.

The tabernacle, thus erected was covered with four different kinds of curtains. The first, or inner curtain was composed of fine linen, magnificently embroidered with figures of cherubim in colors of blue, purple, and scarlet; this formed the beautiful ceiling of the tabernacle. The next covering was made of goats' hair, of a pure white color; the third was of rams' skins dyed red; and the fourth was of badgers' skins. Such was the form and general structure of the tabernacle, and such the coverings by which its sacred furniture was protected from injury by the action of the elements.

Now mark the difference between the inner and the outer of these four curtains. As we enter the Holy Place, which represents the Church of Christ—the curtain which forms the ceiling, and hangs down before us and behind us, in blending shades of blue, purple, and scarlet, is curiously wrought all over with figures of cherubim. This seems to intimate the connection of angels with the Church, and the bright vision disclosed to the view of those who enter it. But look now, in contrast with this, at the outer curtain. It was formed of rough leather. Its appearance was dark and repelling. Yet *that* enveloped the whole structure of the tabernacle, as if to

THE CANDLESTICK. 145

show the aspect which the things of salvation present to those who look at them only from a distance, from an external point of view, and whose eyes have not been opened to behold their hidden beauties, and to see them in the light which shines upon them from the golden candlestick of revelation. The first division of the sanctuary represented the Church on earth; the second division represented the Church in heaven. They were both covered and surrounded by the same curtain, which, as we have seen before, was typical of Christ, as if to teach us that in heaven, as on earth, we shall be alike connected with the righteousness of Christ, as that in which we shall stand, and from which all our happiness shall flow.

But it is time for us to proceed. Well now, let us raise the curtain which hangs at the eastern end of the tabernacle, and enter the Holy Place. A sense of awe may well come over us as we tread within its hallowed precincts, for it is the sanctuary of the Most High,—"the place where His honor dwelleth."

Now, as we stand within this sacred enclosure, three objects meet our view. At the left, on the south side of the Holy Place, stands the golden candlestick, shedding the mild radiance of its heavenly light all through the place. Opposite the candlestick, on the right, stands the table of shew-bread; while before us, and directly in front of the vail which hides from view the Most Holy Place, stands the golden altar of incense. Each of these will, in turn, engage our attention.

We have to do, at present, with *the golden candlestick*. This was made of *solid* gold. The amount of this precious metal employed in the making of it was a talent in weight, according to the Jewish reckoning. This was equivalent to one hundred and twenty-five pounds, Troy weight. At this rate the material employed in the candlestick might be reckoned, in value, at about thirty-five thousand dollars. The exact form and dimensions of it are not given. There is therefore room for difference of opinion in regard to the detail of its arrangements. This difference is seen in the different forms given to its base,—the height assigned it,—and the arrangement of its branches. The seven lamps of the candlestick are sometimes represented as all arranged on the same level; while at other times the lamp on the central shaft is represented as rising higher than the rest. The exact truth on this point cannot now be determined, as nothing is said on the subject in the Scriptures. I prefer to take the latter view of it. We have New Testament authority for considering this candlestick as a figure of the Church. Rev. i. 12, 20. This may aid us in our explanation. But let us examine the different parts of the candlestick. It was composed of a *main shaft, with its connecting branches*. If these branches represent the Church of Christ, the central shaft may well be regarded as representing Christ Himself. As the vine and its branches denote Christ and His people, so the candlestick and its branches may be taken in the same sense. From Christ the Church springs, and by Him it is supported, as the outspreading arms of the candlestick are by its central shaft. The Church is united to Him, and sustained by Him. When the prophet saw in vision, a golden candlestick, with seven lamps, he speaks of a bowl upon the top of it, from which, by pipes, the golden oil was conveyed to the lamps. This idea was not engrafted upon the tabernacle candlestick.

THE CANDLESTICK. 149

But it gives us an interesting illustration of the relation existing between Christ and His people. "Of His fulness they all receive." From Him the golden oil of grace flows down to them. Their life, their strength, their beauty, and their usefulness are all derived from Him.

Notice next the *branches* of the candlestick. These sprang from the central shaft, and were of the same material with each other, and with it. So it is with Christ and His people. "He who sanctifieth, and they who *are* sanctified are all of one." "*As He is, so are we in this world.*" "When He shall appear we shall be like Him." But the shaft was higher than the branches, "for it pleased the Father that, in all things, He,"—Christ—"should have the pre-eminence."

Notice next the *ornaments* upon the candlestick. There were three, viz., *bowls*, *knops*, and *flowers*. There were " bowls like almonds" wrought upon it. In these the branches terminated, forming appropriate receptacles for the lamps of the candlestick. It may be asked why was the almond chosen, both here and in Aaron's rod? The reason is not assigned. It may have been because the almond was the first tree to bud in the spring, which would make it a fit type of Him who is " the first-born from the dead."

The next ornament was the *knops*. What these were is not known. Josephus says they were pomegranates. This was a species of apple. The fruit when ripe was as large as a good-sized orange. Artificial pomegranates were much used as architectural ornaments. These knops, or knobs, may have been swelling buds, from which the branches of the candlestick sprang, expressing the idea that these spreading arms owed both their existence and their fruitfulness to the parent stem.

The other ornaments of the candlestick were the *flowers*. These are natural emblems of beauty. They represent the spiritual loveliness of Christ's people. But the flowers of nature, though surpassingly beautiful, are frail and perishing. But the flowers of grace are all possessed of an amaranthine property. They bloom for immortality. Of this the candlestick gave eloquent intimations in its flowers of *beaten* gold. These flowers wrought in gold, what an interesting figure they furnish of the permanence, or perpetuity that shall characterize the spiritual beauty of the new creation, effected by the grace of God, in Christ Jesus.

Such was the golden candlestick of the Tabernacle, in its form, its structure, and adornments.

We proceed now to consider the lessons which it taught. There are *three* most important lessons taught us by this candlestick. *In the first place, it taught* THE NECESSITY OF A DIVINE REVELATION.

The light which beamed from this candlestick, was derived from heaven. It was the only light, which shone in the tabernacle. There was no window in it. Natural lights, the light of day, never entered or shed its rays there. Suppose the candlestick had been removed, or its lamp left *un*lighted, and we had been introduced into the tabernacle, what would have been our condition? Darkness, like that of Egypt, would have surrounded us. No single ray of light would have relieved the gloom. The hallowed furniture would have been all there in its place. The gorgeous walls of burnished gold would have shut us in, on either side. The variegated curtain with its beautiful tracery of cherubic emblems would have been spread out in silent majesty above our heads. But what the better should we have been for all this lavish expenditure of wealth and beauty? No trace of the loveliness there existing;— no dawning gleam, no faint conception of the rich instruction, the precious treasury of suggestive, saving faith with which that hallowed place was furnished, should we have been able to take in. The light of the outer world could not enter there. Unless then the golden candlestick shed its light upon the surrounding objects, we should have seen nothing, and known nothing of the things that pertain to our salvation.

How eloquently the candlestick thus teaches us the necessity of a divine revelation! Without the light of the candlestick, darkness, the most profound, must have filled the tabernacle. And just such would have been our condition, spiritually considered, without the light of divine revelation. Reason, the natural sun in the mental world, can shed no light upon the soul's concerns. There is no window, in the soul, through which the light of this natural luminary can shine. The priest in the sanctuary could only see his way and discharge his duties by the help of light from the candlestick, and this was light from heaven, a divine revelation. And it is only by the aid of such a revelation that we can see our way in reference to spiritual things. God left the world, for four thousand years, to test the experiment fully, of the power of reason to guide a lost world back to the God from whom it had wandered. The result of that experiment was that "the world by wisdom knew not God." Reason is not to be laid aside when we come to the consideration of spiritual things. There is nothing in this department of knowledge which contradicts the teachings of sound enlightened reason. But in examining the truths of revelation, it is necessary that reason should feel that she is in the presence of a higher power. She should bow her head reverently, as a pupil sitting down at the feet of his master, or as a child coming to a parent for instruction. As the Jewish priest passed from the light of the outer world into the mild radiance shed by the golden candlestick, when he would learn of God and serve Him with acceptance; so we must hold in abeyance the uncertain dictates of unsanctified natural reason, and let our minds be lighted up with the beams which shine from revelation's candlestick, if we would properly understand "the things which accompany salvation." This was the Psalmist's feeling as his reverent Spirit thus expressed itself, while waiting before God: "With Thee is the fountain of life—in *thy* light we shall see light."

The God of the Bible is "the Father of lights." But it is only as He reveals *Himself* that He can be known. Hence said our Saviour, "No man knoweth the Father save the Son, and he to whom the Son shall reveal Him." "The natural man receiveth not the things of the Spirit of God, neither can he know them, because they are spiritually discerned." And thus as we see the golden candlestick, shining in the Holy Place, giving forth the *only light* by which anything can be seen there, we are taught a most impressive lesson respecting the *necessity of divine revelation*.

But, secondly, we are taught here with equal clearness the BENEFITS OF SUCH A REVELATION. We perceive this the moment we look around us, in the Holy Place, and observe what the light of the candlestick discloses to our view. See, over against it stands the golden table with its shew-bread. Twelve loaves of bread stood upon this table, representing the different tribes of Israel. This bread was renewed, from time to time, continually, so as to be always fresh and good. It denoted the plenteousness of God's house, the abundant provision there made for the wants of his people. The loaves upon that table pointed to Christ, the true manna, the bread that came down from heaven. He that eateth of this bread shall live for ever; and shall never hunger for the bread on which others feed. The candlestick, with its heavenly light, enabled the priest, as he entered the Holy Place, to see where to find this bread. He could not have seen it without this light. And so it is only the light of divine revelation which reveals Christ, the heavenly bread, to souls that are hungering and perishing for the want of it. Close your Bible, put out the light which shines from the golden candlestick of divine revelation, and a pall, of thickest darkness, is spread over all the universe. Jesus, the only satisfying portion for the soul, is hidden from view. And no efforts, however persistently made, can reveal Him. Then, indeed, it is true that " none can by searching find Him out—none can know Him" to their satisfaction or salvation. " The sea saith, He is not with me, and the depth saith, He is not in me. He cannot be gotten for gold or silver; for the precious onyx or the sapphire." We often see men rejecting revelation, turning their backs upon the light which shines from God's golden candlestick, and then go groping their way in darkness, through the world of nature, to find a substitute for a rejected Saviour, as the food and portion of their souls. But the experiment, though often made, is always unsuccessful. What an illustrious example of this is furnished in the case of the late Baron Humboldt. He was a modern apostle of the natural sciences. He devoted the energies of his gigantic mind unceasingly to this class of studies. He had ranged through nature in all her departments. He was perfectly familiar with her awful mysteries. He seemed like a walking encyclopedia of this kind of knowledge. But he looked at nature in the light of reason only. Revelation's light he discarded. Did he succeed in finding a substitute for Christ as the bread from heaven, the satisfying portion of his soul? We have our answer in one of his heart-utterances breathed into the ear of an intimate friend not long before his death. *"I live a joyless life"* was his acknowledgment. How instructive, how affecting! Here is a man with all the treasures of knowledge, connected with earthly sciences, poured out at his feet, and all the honors that emanate from earthly sources heaped upon his head—and yet "in the midst of his sufficiencies he is in straits." "I live a joyless life" is the sorrowful sighing of his unsatisfied spirit. Contrast this with the experience of those who, walking in the light of God's golden candlestick, have found Christ, the bread from heaven, and live continually on Him. When their experience takes form and clothes itself with language, it finds expression, thus:

> "From pole to pole, let others roam,
> And search in vain for bliss;
> Our souls are satisfied at home;
> The Lord our portion is.
>
> His word of promise is our food;
> His Spirit is our guide;
> Thus daily is our strength renew'd
> And all our wants supplied."

The difference between these two classes of persons may be all expressed by the different termination given to the adjective which qualifies their lives. Baron Humboldt representing one class, said, "I live a joy*less* life." Any true Christian representing the other would say, "I live a joy*ful* life." As pointing out the bread upon the table in the sanctuary—the satisfying provision made for the wants of God's people, the candlestick in the tabernacle illustrated *the benefits of divine revelation.*

But turn now from the table of shewbread, and see, directly in front of us, stands the golden altar of incense. Fragrant odors are rising from it. This points to the acceptance of the prayers of God's people, through the prevailing efficacy of the sacrifice of Christ. The candlestick revealed this in the tabernacle. And that which the golden altar and its incense typified, viz., the way of acceptance with God for guilty sinners, the light of revelation alone discloses. Where else can you go and find a satisfactory answer to the question—"How shall man be just with God?" You hear some anxious soul, oppressed and burdened under a sense of sin, propounding the momentous inquiry—"Wherewithal shall I come before the Lord, and bow myself before the Most High?" But *reason* can suggest no solution to the important problem. History, philosophy, observation, and experience, though gathered from all the outspreadings of the globe, apart from the Bible and its teachings, can throw no light upon it. But bring the question up to where revelation shines, and it is resolved at once. A way of access to the mercy-seat, through the infinite merits of the sacrifice of Christ is clearly manifested. Through Him, the prayers, the persons, and the services of His people all find acceptance.

And then, observe the light which shone from the candlestick *disclosed itself to view*. We read that "it gave light over against it." The candlestick represented the mystery of Christ and His Church. It was a beautiful illustration of the union existing between Jesus and His ransomed people, and of their participation in the glorious blessings of His grace. But, it was only the light dispensed by the lamps on the candlestick which could bring this out to view. Yes, it was this which revealed all that beautiful tracery of fruits and flowers which appeared on that golden, central shaft. That shaft represents Christ. That graceful adornment with which it is covered over, points out the wonders of His love, the riches of His grace, the treasured sweetness of His saving name, in His covenant relation to His people. And all this can only be seen by the light of revelation, as it shines in the sanctuary. And it is this unfolding of the preciousness of Christ which constitutes the glory of God's house. The excellency of the knowledge of Jesus is displayed there. It is the place of His manifestation. The Bible is, throughout, " the book of the revelation of Jesus Christ." It was this unfolding of His character which constituted " the power and glory" of God, which the Psalmist had seen in the sanctuary, and which he so earnestly desired again to see. And it is this which makes the sanctuary seem, to the believer, to be so often like what the cleft rock in the mountain side was to Moses,—and what Patmos, with its visions of glory, was to St. John,— the very vestibule of heaven. And when we look round on all these objects, as disclosed to us in the Holy Place by the light of the candlestick, then in the good things of which these were the shadows we learn our lesson of *the benefits of a divine revelation.*

We look to the candlestick, for the third

THE CANDLESTICK.   165

lesson which it teaches us, that is, the PERFECTION OF THIS REVELATION.

This is taught us by the number of lamps which it bore. There were *seven* of these. This number denotes completeness or perfection. In the Apocalyptic vision of heaven which St. John had, he saw—" seven lamps of fire burning before the throne, which are the seven spirits of God." This language refers to the Holy Ghost, the third person in the adorable Trinity. It denotes that blessed Spirit in the exercise of his omnipotent and perfect influences. This is referred to in the hymn incorporated into our ordination service. Thus it reads:

> "Come, Holy Ghost, our souls inspire,
> And lighten with celestial fire.
> Thou, the anointing Spirit art,
> Who dost thy *seven-fold* gifts impart."

The lamps burning on the golden candlestick, with the heavenly light they imparted, were a type or emblem of this Spirit. All the light which shone in the Jewish tabernacle emanated from those lamps; and so all the light, in reference to divine things, which shines in the Christian Sanctuary comes from the Holy Ghost. He is the "Lord and Giver of light." He is the Author of revelation. All the radiance which it sheds around the pathway of the redeemed proceeds from Him. And His light is perfect. The natural light, which beams around us continually, in all its varying beauty is made up, we know, of the seven primary colors. Its seven-fold nature makes it perfect. And so it is with the light of revelation, the light which the Holy Ghost sheds on the things that relate to our salvation. This is a seven-fold, or perfect light. It is not perfect in its degree, now; but it is entirely perfect in its kind. His light is sufficient to supply the wants of all believers, and to finish in their souls every work he begins there. And while He acts differently on each individual, sanctifying all, yet He makes no two exactly alike. "For as the sunbeam, when it falls upon the landscape, draws forth a thousand shades, of which each is beautiful, and yet all are different, so the Spirit of God, shining in the midst of the people of Christ, colors each soul with a peculiar grace, while rendering all partakers, by degrees, of advancing, complete, and universal holiness."

"At one time He manifests Himself as a Spirit of wisdom. He gives skill, knowledge, counsel. Thus He inspired Bezaleel to build the tabernacle. Thus also 'Joshua was full of the Spirit of wisdom, for Moses had laid his hands upon him.' This means that he was full of the Spirit of God. And so Christ himself, receiving for us the Holy Ghost in all His fulness, had resting on Him 'the spirit of wisdom and understanding.' It is a delightful thought that He does so manifest Himself. Who does not feel again and again, his need of wisdom. Here is an ever-burning lamp."

"Sometimes he manifests himself as a Spirit of might. Hence St. Paul prays that the Ephesians may be "strengthened with might by his spirit in the inner man. Wisdom would avail us little without strength. Our own strength is perfect weakness; but all in whom the Spirit of God dwells, 'out of weakness are made strong.'"

"Again he reveals himself as a Spirit of truth. The peculiar office of the Spirit is to testify of Jesus, and to lead the believer to know more and more of his excellency and glory. The Bible is the Spirit's book. No heavenly truths are known to man without his illumination. All the light of the

Church is from the lamp of the Spirit. Christ himself, in promising the Comforter, three times calls him the Spirit of truth. And just in proportion as we have the Spirit, will be our real, profitable knowledge of divine truth. "He leadeth into all truth." "The Spirit searcheth all things, yea, the deep things of God."

"He is the Spirit of promise. The gift of the Spirit is the promise of Christ to all that believe on him. And the Spirit having given the promises of scripture, applies them to the heart. He enables the believer to grasp the promises, and use them for the supply of his own individual necessities. And thus, it is through the Spirit's influence that he is able to preserve his serenity amid trial and temptation."

"He is the Spirit of adoption. Entering into the bosom of the believer he gives him a son-like feeling. The Christian, through the indwelling Spirit, learns to look upon God as his Father. He no longer stands at a distance from Him; his very sins, which he would be ashamed to tell to any one else, he pours forth with more than filial confidence, into the bosom of Jehovah; and as an adopted child, he makes it his grand object to walk worthy of so gracious a Father. Thus believers receive the Spirit of adoption whereby they cry—Abba Father."

"In short, he is the Spirit of grace,—the one only source of all holiness,—the author of everything in the believer's conduct that is really good,—the great Sanctifier, and also the Spirit of glory, fitting the people of Christ for the enjoyment of that heaven which is already theirs by right, and even now throwing around them, when at their best, a brightness of holiness before which all worldly glory 'pales its ineffectual light.'"

" There is also endless variety in the gifts which the Spirit bestows on different individuals. All are not Bezaleels, endued with special talents for the edifying of the Church; nor Joshuas, full of wisdom and vigor to do great things in the cause of Christ. The same Spirit gave prudence to James, and energy to Paul, and winning gentleness to John, though once the son of thunder. He gives different *gifts* to different individuals, according to the different works he has planned for them. And even his graces are not bestowed in like measure upon all. He lighted up more self-denying devotedness in Paul than in all the other apostles. He filled Peter with most of zeal, and perhaps least of firmness. And if we knew more of the individual characters of the rest of the apostles, we should find in each some grace marked with especial strength. It will be so even in heaven.

The lamps of fire are seven there. The Spirit's grace though abundant for all, will be given according to the need of each. And thus, throughout eternity, there will be a blessed harmony arising from the union of different holy characters. There will still be Peters, and Pauls, and Johns, all perfect, but not all alike. The members of Christ will still have their several offices. The trees in the heavenly paradise,—the jewels in the Jerusalem that is above,—will not be all the same. "One star will differ from another star in glory." The harps of gold will sound in harmony, but not in unison. There will be variety there, as there is here. "But all these worketh that one and the self-same Spirit, dividing to every man severally as He will." (Garrett's Scripture Symbolism.)

And when we look upon the candlestick, with its seven-fold light, we see beautifully

THE CANDLESTICK. 173

illustrated, the perfection of divine revelation as exhibited in the Spirit's work on the hearts and in the lives of God's people.

The necessity of divine revelation; the benefits of divine revelation; and *the perfection of divine revelation;* these are the lessons taught us by the golden candlestick.

In conclusion, *what cause for thankfulness this subject suggests that our connection is not with the candlestick as it was a shadow, but with the substance which that shadow represents!* The golden candlestick, in the Jewish Church, was a great blessing to those who lived under that dispensation; but ah! *that* was as nothing compared to the light which we enjoy, as it shines from the seven golden candlesticks of the Christian Church, in the midst of which the glorious Saviour walks continually! The light of the Jewish candlestick was a *local* light. It was confined to a single spot. It shone within the precincts of the tabernacle, but it shone no where else. Those who desired to avail themselves of its benefits must journey up thither; but when they returned home they must leave that light behind them. It could not shine upon them in their own dwellings. Earth's weary pilgrims, in other lands, groping their way in darkness through this fallen world, could not be cheered, or comforted by that light. But the light of the Christian candlestick is not local. It is " a light to lighten the Gentiles," while yet the glory of God's people, Israel.

> "The beams that shine from Zion's hill
> Shall lighten *every* land."

It is light from the Sun of Righteousness. This sun will rise higher and higher till the whole earth shall be bathed in the radiance of His glory. And yet while capable of this universal diffusion, it has the power of penetrating and pervading the minds of all God's people; so that they can apply to themselves the language of the apostle and say, that "God, who commanded the light out of darkness hath *shined in our hearts* to give the light of the knowledge of the glory of God in the face of Jesus Christ."

The light of the Jewish candlestick was *stationary*. What it was on the first day on which its lamps were lighted, *that* it was the next day, and so on during all the days of its continuance. Its radiance might reach a certain point, but it never could exceed it. It was not capable of increase. But it is very different with the light of the Christian candlestick. This is not stationary, but progressive. No limit can be fixed to the brightness of its shining. In breadth of circle, in fulness of volume, in clearness of ray, there is room for unceasing increase.

Through all the years of time, through all the ages of eternity, it will be a growing light, "shining more and more unto the perfect day."

The light of the Jewish candlestick was a *temporary* light. It was liable, at any time, to be extinguished, and was finally put out. Not so with the light of the Christian candlestick. This is an abiding, inextinguishable, everlasting light. All the efforts and malice of wicked men and wicked spirits, singly or combined, can no more extinguish this light in a single soul, where it has been once kindled by the omnipotence of sovereign grace, than they can stop the stars from shining, or pluck the sun from its orbit. O, have we not a glorious *substance* in this light? and is it not cause for thankfulness to be connected with this, rather than the shadowy shining of the former dispensation?

Further, *the subject before us is very instructive in the suggestions it furnishes as to the practical character God's people should bear.* We see this in the beautiful tracery of the candlestick. It was covered, all over, with golden flowers, and golden fruit. This intimated that God's people were to be a *flower-decked, fruit-bearing* people. They are distinguished by the beautifying graces of the Holy Spirit, fitly represented by flowers, and by the substantial *fruits* of holy living. And it is interesting to see how God caused to be inwrought upon the golden candlestick, of that shadowy dispensation, a symbol clearly expressive of this idea. If any are inclined to think this a fanciful construction, let me quote here the remarks of President Edwards, one of the ablest theologians the Church ever knew. His gigantic mind was not likely to be misled by fancies. "The Candlestick," says he, "was like a tree of many branches, and bearing flowers and fruit, agreeably to the very frequent representations of the Church, by a tree, a vine, a grain of mustard-seed. In this candlestick every flower is attended with a knop, an apple, or pomegranate, representing a good profession attended with a corresponding fruit in God's people. Here were rows of knops and flowers one after another, beautifully representing the progress of Christians in religious attainments, their going from strength to strength. Such is the nature of true grace, that it bears flowers that promise a further degree of fruit, the flowers having in them the principle of new fruit, and by this progress in holiness believers come to shine as lights in the world."

And then observe that the tracery on the branches of the candlestick is precisely the same as that upon the central shaft. This shaft, we have seen, represents Christ. The branches represent his people. Would you know if you are a true branch of the spiritual candlestick? Look if you can find in your heart and life, the same beautiful tracery of the Spirit's work which appeared in the heart and life of Jesus. The same flowers of spiritual loveliness, the same fruits of practical holiness, in kind, though not in degree, is the only satisfactory proof of discipleship. To be a Christian is to be like Jesus. He left us an example that we should follow his steps. Let all our hearts go out in the earnest prayer,

> "Thy fair example may we trace,
> To teach us what we ought to be;
> Make us, by thy transforming grace,
> O Savior, daily more like Thee!"

Beloved hearers, who are not Christians, you walk in darkness. Yes, darkness is within you—darkness is around you. The

shadow of death has settled down upon you.
O come out from this shadow. The true
light is now shining from the cross of Christ.

> "O look to Jesus, and you'll find
>   In Him your Star, your Sun,
> And in that light of life you'll walk
>   Till travelling days are done."

I love to linger in the rays of this glorious
Light of the world. Let me close, however,
with quoting the beautiful lines of one who
thus points us away from the shadows of
the past dispensation to the substance of the
present:

"The last star has set, and the Sun in his splendor
  From the chambers of day in his majesty springs!
And a gold-dropping glory, by mercy made tender,
  Distils on the faint, from His far-spreading wings!

He comes in his grace, and he comes in his beauty,
  To brighten man's darkest, and drear'est abode,
To shine on the fields and the deserts of duty,—
  To light up the pathway that leads us to God.

Behold! how his rays on the mountains are sparkling
    The shadows of midnight are lost to our view.
Shout, nations! no more shall you wander all darkling
    For the 'Light of the world" beameth brightly on you.

He will light you through toil, he will light you through sorrow ;
    He will beam on your journey, and smile on your grave;
He will wake up your souls to an unsetting morrow ;
    For the 'Light of the world' is all-powerful to save ?"

CHAPTER V.

The Table of Shew-Bread.

"Thou shalt also make a table of shittim-wood: two cubits shall be the length thereof, and a cubit the breadth thereof, and a cubit and a half the height thereof. And thou shalt overlay it with pure gold, and make thereto a crown of gold round about. And thou shalt make unto it a border of an hand breadth round about, and thou shalt make a golden crown to the border thereof round about. And thou shalt make for it four rings of gold, and put the rings in the four corners that are on the four feet thereof. Over against the border shall the rings be for places of the staves to bear the table. And thou shalt make the staves of shittim-wood, and overlay them with gold, that the table may be borne with them. And thou shalt make the dishes thereof, and spoons thereof, and covers thereof, and bowls thereof, to cover withal: of pure gold shalt thou make them. And thou shalt set upon the table shew-bread before me alway."—EXODUS, xxv. 23—30.

THE TABLE OF SHEW BREAD.
Jewish Tabernacle.

V.

We imagine ourselves to be standing just within the vail which hangs down over the eastern end of the Tabernacle. We have crossed the threshold of the Holy Place. The golden candlestick, which we last considered, is shedding its hallowed light on all around us. Over against this candlestick, stands the table of Shew-bread. This is the next article in the furniture of the tabernacle that we are to consider. It is so full of instruction, so replete with lessons of practical interest, that, without any prefatory remarks, we proceed, at once, to notice the structure of this table, and the important truths it illustrates for our edification.

Look now at the form and structure of this table. Like the ark itself, it was composed of acacia wood overlaid with pure gold. It was a plain, simple table, without any of the ornamental work, or curious tracery, with which the candlestick was covered all over. There was a border of a hand's breadth surrounding it. This was designed, it is supposed, for the golden vessels connected with the table to stand upon. There was also a rim, or crown of gold, inside of this border, intended, no doubt, to keep the loaves in their places, and prevent their being disturbed, in the constant journeyings of the people through the wilderness.

In its dimensions this table was three feet in length, eighteen inches in breadth, and twenty-seven inches in height. There were rings, at the corners, beneath the border, through which the staves were put for carrying it.

THE TABLE OF SHEW-BREAD. 187

On this table were placed loaves of bread. These loaves were unleavened bread, made out of fine flour. In number these loaves were twelve, corresponding to the different tribes of Israel. They were placed in two parallel rows, not piled up on each other, as you sometimes see them represented, but ranging horizontally, the length of the table. The loaves were renewed every Sabbath, so as to be always fresh. When placed upon the table the surface of the loaves was covered over with a layer of powdered frankincense. This was a pure white powder which would give to the loaves an appearance somewhat resembling the frosted cakes of modern confectioners. When the old loaves were removed this powdered frankincense was gathered into one of the golden dishes connected with the table, and burned before the Lord "as an offering made by fire." The loaves, when taken from the table, were reserved for the use of Aaron and his sons. "It was not lawful for any to eat of them but the priests only." Luke vi. 4.

These are all the particulars furnished us by the sacred writers respecting the table of shew-bread. No explanation is given, in the scripture narrative, of the meaning of this part of the furniture of the tabernacle. In attempting to point out this meaning, it does not become us to dogmatize, or deal in positive assertion. It rather becomes us to tread reverently here, as Moses did at the burning bush, when he "put off the shoes from his feet, because the ground on which he stood was holy ground." We are not at liberty, out of a type, or figure, to weave an argument by which to set forth a truth not elsewhere clearly taught in scripture. The only legitimate use to make of the types and figures of the Old Testament, is to set them forth as illustrations of truths revealed in other parts of the volume of revelation. There is no difficulty whatever in attempting to make such a use of the Table of Shewbread. It affords us beautiful illustrations of God's precious truth, as we find the same revealed in the pages of the New Testament. Let us proceed now to consider the lessons which it teaches.

And the first lesson we learn here is taught us by THE NATURE OF THE BREAD UPON THE TABLE.

This we know, on the very best authority, was a symbol of Christ. Jesus taught us this distinctly and clearly when He said, " I am the bread of life." That bread upon the table points to Jesus. How apt a type, or emblem of Him, it was! *The bread was a prepared substance.* It was not a natural growth. Forethought and design were employed in the production of it. And so it was with Christ. His mysterious being was not a thing of natural growth. It was the result of God's infinite wisdom,—the product of His everlasting purpose, or plan. Hence said Jesus, anticipating His incarnation, and contemplating Himself, from this very point of view,—"A body hast Thou *prepared* me."

But that bread was a *compound* substance, and in this aspect of it, how significantly it pointed to Christ. The flour alone could never have been formed into those loaves which stood upon the golden table in the tabernacle. Another element was necessary. Water must be mingled and blended with the flour, and then it must be exposed to the action of fire, or it never could have been made into bread. And it was just so with Christ. He had been a partaker of the divine nature from eternity. But this, of itself, would never have qualified Him to be our Redeemer. *One* nature, alone, could not

THE TABLE OF SHEW-BREAD. 191

have enabled Him to become "the bread of life" to a famishing world. If possessed *only* of the divine nature, or only of the human nature, He never could have met the necessities of our case. He must be a *compound* being to do this. And so He took our nature upon Him, and then passed through the fire of suffering that He might be a perfect Saviour. He blended the humanity with the divinity. And thus he was enabled to say of Himself—" I am the bread that came down from heaven."

That bread, upon the table, was a *necessary* substance. Without it the Jewish priest would have had no strength for the performance of his sacred functions, and no enjoyment in any of the privileges of the sanctuary. His feeble frame would have fainted and failed, but for the support which this afforded him. And just so necessary Jesus is to the life and comfort of His people.

He could say, authoritatively, to the Jews when on earth, and the saying is as true now as it was then, "Except ye eat the flesh of the Son of Man, and drink His blood, ye have no life in you." It is not only a *pleasant* thing, a *desirable* thing, an *important* thing for our souls to eat of this bread—but in the strongest and most absolute sense, i is a *necessary* thing.

And then the bread upon that table was as *suitable* as it was necessary. It was wonderfully adapted to meet all the physical wants of the priest who partook of it. It adapted itself entirely to all the cravings of his feeble frame. It furnished the whole of his complex system with the nourishment it required. As he partook of it he felt life and vigor pervade every part of his body. And just what bread is to the body, in this respect, Christ is to the soul. His people *live* on Him. They have an appropriating principle, a power of assimilation that applies to every aspect and particle of "the truth as it is in Jesus." It is quickening truth, sustaining truth, enlightening truth, comforting, sanctifying, and saving truth.

And then, moreover, that bread upon the golden table was *unleavened* bread. Leaven in Scripture was the symbol of error, or corruption. Hence we find St. Paul speaking of "the leaven of malice and wickedness." Satan has been allowed to enter the Church, in its outward organization, and to spread the leaven of error and corruption through all its departments. But he has never been allowed to touch the *bread* of the Christian tabernacle. This has always remained,— what the Jewish type, or figure of it was,— unleavened bread. Jesus, whom that bread represented, has continued unchanged from the beginning. The testimony of Scripture concerning Him is, that He is "the *same* yesterday, to-day, and forever." " In Him is no darkness at all." He is truth without any admixture of error. He is purity without the slightest taint of corruption.

But, though without leaven *in Himself*, He may be received, and held, in a way that will make Him, *to us*, as though He were bread that is leavened. This will always be the case when He is not received, and held, in the simplicity and completeness of His covenant relation to His people. "Christ is the substance of all true doctrine; all doctrine in which anything else is mixed up with Christ as the ground of dependence is false. Any view of the gospel which makes Christ *and* natural goodness,— Christ *and* good works, —Christ *and* the sacraments,—Christ *and* inward experience,—Christ *and* anything else, the ground of a sinner's hope of acceptance with God is a false view of it." This is attempting to *leaven* the bread of the Sanc-

THE TABLE OF SHEW-BREAD. 195

tuary. Christ must be *everything* to His people, or He will be nothing to them. And thus, from the nature of the bread upon the golden table we get our first lesson.

Our second lesson is furnished by observing THE WAY IN WHICH THIS BREAD WAS MANIFESTED. Two things were required to this end, viz., the light which shone from the golden candlestick, and the table to lift up, or elevate the bread so that it could be distinctly seen. If the candlestick were not lighted, and casting forth its illuminating beams, the bread might be upon the table, but darkness would envelope it. The officiating priest could never see it. And so it is only the light of revelation, the illuminating influence of the Holy Ghost, which can make manifest Christ, the true bread from heaven, to the souls of famishing sinners. But this thought was so fully developed in our last discourse that we need not enlarge upon it here.

Yet, even when the candlestick was lighted, and shedding its mild radiance through the Holy Place, the services of the table were needed for the shewing, or making manifest of the bread. And hence the name applied to it,—"the table of *shew*-bread." The design of this table was plain and simple. It had but *one* office to fulfill. It had its being, and its place, in the Sanctuary, for the single purpose of lifting-up, exhibiting, making manifest, or setting forth, the bread which was placed upon it. And here the question naturally arises, of what is this table itself a figure or type? What does it represent in the Christian Church? But, in order to answer this question satisfactorily, it is necessary to ask another. What is there in the Christian Church, which accomplishes an object analogous to that sub-

THE TABLE OF SHEW-BREAD. 197

served by this table in the Jewish tabernacle? The one design of the golden table, we have seen, was to lift up the hallowed bread, and present it to view, continually. But this bread represented Christ. And in the Christian Church, we know, the agency appointed of God for exhibiting, holding forth, or making Christ manifest to perishing men is the office of the ministry. And thus we seem authorized, nay, *compelled* to regard the golden table, which held the shew-bread, in the tabernacle, as beautifully representing to us, in symbol, *the design, or purpose of the Christian ministry.*

Now this view of the matter furnishes us with some striking and valuable suggestions. Observe this table was a *golden* table. This denoted its value. It was thus like the candlestick, whose majestic shaft, with its beautiful tracery of the same precious metal, represented Christ. So, the minister of the gospel, to be able to execute his office rightly, must, by the power of transforming grace, be made like unto the Son of God. To be a true minister, he must be conformed to the image of Christ by being "created anew in Christ Jesus." As the wood of the table was overlaid with pure gold, to fit it for the position it was to occupy in the tabernacle, so the corrupt nature of the minister of the gospel must be covered over with that fine gold of the Sanctuary, the converting, sanctifying grace of God, before he can be made, in this respect, "a vessel sanctified and meet for the Master's service."

Again, the *pure gold* which overspread this table denoted the *honor and dignity of the service in which it was to be employed.* Its place was in the Sanctuary. Like Gabriel its high privilege was "to stand in the presence of God." The bread spread out upon it was called "the bread of the *pres-*

ence," because it was presented continually before the face of the Most High. And so the honor, or dignity of the office of the ministry, lies in this, that all its duties and services connect themselves, directly, with God. The minister is God's herald, or ambassador. He is the servant of Jesus Christ. He hears the word at His mouth, and warns men from Him. It was in this view of the trust committed to him, that Paul rejoiced in his portion, and "*magnified* his office."

But notice the *simplicity* and *plainness* of this table. What a contrast it presented, in this respect, to the candlestick, which stood over against it! *That* was covered all over with its curious wreathen work, its golden, glorious tracery of buds, and flowers, and fruit; while this was required to be without embellishment or ornament of any kind. Nor can we wonder at this. The candlestick represented Christ, in the glory of His own infinite fulness and sufficiency. It is right and proper that He should attract to Himself the admiring gaze of all His people. Hence the elaborate work upon the candlestick. But the table was only a subordinate agency, employed to exhibit the shew-bread. It was not the purpose of God that it should attract attention to itself. Hence plainness and simplicity marked it. All its significance, and all its importance, lay in the hallowed burden which it bore,—the consecrated bread which it held up to the gaze of all who entered the Holy Place.

In every rightly constructed sentence there is some one word which brings out the meaning of the passage. A skilful elocutionist will throw all his emphasis into that word. He will do this, partly, by the increased *stress* laid upon that word, and partly, by keeping down, and making unemphatic the other words in the sentence. God built the tabernacle on this principle. Take the portion of it now before us, as an illustration. The table of shew-bread is a symbolical sentence, rightly constructed. The one word which brings out the meaning of this sentence is *the bread*. God made this word emphatic, by the stress laid upon it, the prominence assigned it. At the same time he added vastly to the force of that emphasis by keeping down the other parts of the sentence, *i. e.*, by the utter plainness of the table itself. What a lesson this teaches to the ministers of the gospel! How significantly it enjoins them, to "preach *not themselves*, but Christ Jesus, the Lord." If the gospel be compressed into a single sentence, the emphatic words connected with it will be—*Jesus Christ and Him crucified*. Whatever the gifts, or attainments of a minister be, they should all be employed, "first, last, midst, and without end" in giving emphasis to these words. He should give them all the prominence, and lay upon them all the stress in his power. And in aiming to do this, he should keep down everything else, and *especially keep down himself*. What the bread was to the table, that Christ should be to the minister. The minister is nothing. Christ is everything. The object of the ministry is to hold up Christ, and make Him known. The meaning, the dignity, the power, the worth of the ministry, depend on the clearness and faithfulness with which it exhibits Christ to men. And this lesson we are taught when we see the golden table, in its plainness, and utter absence of ornament, as it were, hiding itself beneath the glorious symbol of Christ, the hallowed bread which it ever presented to view.

We look at this table again, and the third

lesson it teaches us is suggested by THE ABUNDANCE OF THE SUPPLY *placed upon it.*

The table bore *twelve* loaves. There was one for each of the tribes. No part of God's family was overlooked, or neglected, in the symbolical provision thus made for their necessities. And what was true, in this respect, of the symbol, is equally true of the thing symbolised. When the prodigal son came to himself, amidst the want and desolation that stared him in the face, he said: "In my Father's house is bread enough, and to spare." And every famishing soul may see this, in returning to God through penitence and faith in Christ. In the broadest and fullest sense, it is true, spiritually considered, that " in our Father's house there is bread enough, and to spare."

Jesus, whom the bread upon the golden table represented, is an infinite Savior. The resources of His sufficiency are exhaustless.

Look at yonder son. How striking an emblem, or representative he is of Christ in this respect! See, how like a god, he pours forth unceasingly his beams of light! For six thousand years he has been doing this, without a moment's *intercession*. No power of human or angelic arithmetic can calculate the number of his rays. And yet, so far from being exhausted, he is just as full of power to shine, and bless, a benighted universe now as in the day of his creation. And so it is with Christ. Infinity pertains to every view we can take of his character, and every relation he sustains to his people. His love, his wisdom, his power, his grace his goodness are all infinite. And infinite too is the atoning efficacy of His sacrifice. It is derogatory to His character that we should apply measures and guages to the infinitude of His fulness. There is no limit to the worth and efficacy of His great sacri-

THE TABLE OF SHEW-BREAD. 205

fice. And there is no limit either to the stores of His sufficiency, when considered as the bread of life to His people. The twelve loaves upon the golden table of the tabernacle were indeed a definite number, but they were designed to represent that which is indefinite.

" Christ, the true bread," says an English writer, " is sufficient for the wants of all. His sacrifice was made for all the tribes of earth, and for each individual of every tribe. The everlasting purpose was—' that he, by the grace of God should taste death for *every man.*' Heb. ii. 9. His love and His redemption were alike without limit. He ' willeth all men to be saved,' and therefore ' he gave himself a ransom for all.' 1 Tim. ii. 6. Those strangely mistake the matter, who would shut up the mercy of our God, as willing to save, within the narrow limits into which man's perverseness in refusing to be saved has drawn it, and count the Saviour's blood a ransom enough for the few who are saved, but too small for the multitudes who perish. This is not to exalt the grace of God, but to debase it. Is this the way of God's dealings? Does He not clothe with grass and with flowers vast tracts which no eye ever rests upon? Does He not scatter the fruits of the earth, in endless profusion, even where there are none to enjoy them? Does He not shower down His rain on the desert? and His sunbeams on the deep? And is it likely, is it possible, that God, who is so liberal, so lavish as the God of creation, should shut up his hand, and contract his bounty, as the God of grace? that when drawing forth out of the depths of His Infinite love, a plan for the redemption of ruined man, and so bent upon it, as not to spare His own dear Son, but to give Him up for the purpose—is it possible that He

THE TABLE OF SHEW-BREAD. 207

should calculate and weigh out, and adjust with scrupulous accuracy the worth of the blood of Jesus, so that it should just be, to a fraction, a commercial equivalent for the sins of His elect people, but neither more, nor less? No. "He died for all." 2 Cor. v. 15. As quaint old Henry Wotton expresses it:—

> "One rosy drop from David's seed
> Was worlds of seas to quench God's ire."

In our Father's house, there is "bread enough, and to spare." This lesson is suggested to us by the abundance of the supply of bread upon the golden table.

We look to this table again and we are taught a lesson by the TIME FOR THE RENEWING *of the bread upon it.*

By an ordinance of God this was always to be done upon the Sabbath. And seeing that the renewing of it was to be weekly there was a manifest propriety in connecting it with this hallowed day. Thus God would put honor upon the Sabbath, and associate it, in the minds of His people, with the thought of obtaining the supply of their spiritual necessities. One circumstance connected with this matter may indeed excite surprise. The supply of manna which was given to Israel with unvarying regularity on every other day of the week was suspended on the Sabbath, while the loaves upon the table of shew-bread, never given on any other day of the week, were always furnished fresh on this particular day. The question naturally arises *why* was this? No explanation is given in the scriptures. We may venture a suggestion respecting it. The manna took the place of the daily bread of the people, the supply of their temporal wants, ordinarily procured as the result of *their own* labor; it would seem proper, there-

THE TABLE OF SHEW-BREAD.

fore, that the supply of this should be interrupted on the day on which they were not allowed to pursue their wonted avocations. But the loaves upon the golden table represented Christ, the true bread which came down from heaven. This was not to be obtained by any work or labor done by men. It was bread sent down from heaven, of God's own free grace and goodness. It was equally proper, therefore, that the giving of this should be connected with the day that was specially set apart for the solemn worship of God. And thus this weekly renewal of the bread upon the golden table on the Sabbath pointed to the ministrations of the sanctuary. These pertain peculiarly to that day which God hallowed to His own special service. And what is the design of these sacred ministrations but to supply God's sanctuary with that spiritual bread which the necessities of His people require?

And this is done effectually when Jesus is clearly and faithfully held forth to men, in the fulness and freeness of His great salvation. When His character is unfolded—when His truth is explained—when His love is made known—when His covenant is laid open—and the sweetness of His saving name is revealed, then indeed "the bread which came down from heaven" is set forth anew on the table of the Christian sanctuary; and those who tread its courts possess the substance, of which the table of shew-bread in the Jewish tabernacle was the shadow.

But a shadow affords only an imperfect representation of the substance which forecasts it. All figures fail adequately to represent the fulness of blessing that we enjoy in Christ. The figure before us fails in *this*. The supply of bread for the Jewish tabernacle was a periodical supply. It was furnished only once a week. But it is not so with us. Jesus, our bread from heaven, has "all seasons for his own." He is set forth, indeed, most formally, and fully on the Sabbath, but not exclusively then. He may be set forth at any time. In season and out of season His ministers are required to "hold forth the word of life." At all times, in all places, and under all circumstances, they are authorised and expected to set forth on God's table that bread of life, of which when any man eateth he shall live forever.

In looking once more at the golden table we learn a lesson from the continual FRESHNESS *of the bread set out upon it.*

This bread as we have seen was renewed every week. It was never permitted to grow old, so as to become stale and unfit for use. There was *fresh* bread upon the table from year to year, from generation to generation. This was beautifully significant of what God's spiritual Israel find fully realized in Christ. The constantly renewed loaves, and the ever repeated sacrifices, of the Mosaic dispensation, were practical and most powerful arguments in proof of the *imperfection* of those services. But Christ, our bread from heaven, never grows old. It needs no renewing. We want no other food for the support and nourishment of our souls. We crave no change in Jesus. As He is now, as He has been from the beginning, He is "all our salvation and all our desire." The language of our hearts, in reference to Him, is, "Lord, evermore, give us *this* bread." The bread furnished in the Christian sanctuary is always fresh, always new, always pleasant and satisfying. As Israel wandered through the wilderness they often were tired of the manna on which they fed there. They murmured at its sameness. The language of their repining was: " Our souls *loathe*

THE TABLE OF SHEW-BREAD. 213

this light bread." But the spiritual Israel have no such experience. They are often weary of other things; they grow weary of themselves—weary of their sins and sorrows, and weary of the world and its vanities—but they never, never grow weary of Jesus. Having once eaten of the bread which He gives, which He *constitutes*, it is literally true that they "never hunger" for the husks the world can offer. There is a satisfying element in this bread which the soul feels, and rejoices in, to the very centre of its being. As believers live by faith on Jesus, it is the language of genuine experience to which they give utterance, when they say of Him;

> "His person fixes all our love,
> His blood removes our fear;
> And while He pleads for us above,
> His arm preserves us here.
>
> His word of promise is our food,
> His spirit is our guide;

> Thus daily is our strength renew'd,
> *And all our wants supplied.*"

But, no abstract description of the properties of ordinary bread will give us a true knowledge of it, till we taste and partake of it ourselves, and so it is emphatically with this heavenly bread. Those who have never had personal experience of the preciousness of Christ cannot believe the report of Him which his people give. They are ready to ask of Him, as the friends of the spouse, in book of Canticles asked of her:—" What is thy beloved, more than any other beloved ?" And if like the spouse we answer: " Our Beloved is the chief among ten thousand, and altogether lovely"—this will not carry conviction. Therefore we say to the hungry and famishing,—" O, taste " this heavenly bread, and see for yourselves what its preciousness is! When you have done this,

THE TABLE OF SHEW-BREAD.

you will know how fresh, how satisfying this bread is! Then each of you will be ready to say—

> "Of Him who did salvation bring,
>   I could forever think and sing;
> When with His name I'm charm'd in song,
>   I wish myself all ear, all tongue.
>
> O let me ever share His grace,
>   Still taste His love, and view His face!
> Still let my tongue resound His name,
>   And *Jesus* be my constant theme.
>
> Blest Saviour! what delicious fare!
>   How sweet thy entertainments are!
> Never did angels taste above,
>   Redeeming grace and dying love!"

And this sweet lesson we have shadowed forth in the *freshness* of the bread placed upon the golden table of the Tabernacle.

We take one more look at this table, and gather our sixth and last lesson from THE COVERING OF FRANKINCENSE WHICH WE SEE SPREAD OUT OVER THE TOP OF THE BREAD.

The direction given respecting this part of the service of the table was in these words :—" And thou shalt put pure frankincense upon each row, that it may be on the bread for a memorial, even an offering made by fire unto the Lord." Lev. xxiv. 7. This frankincense was an aromatic gum, which, when pulverised, yielded a beautiful, pure, white powder. This was placed upon the table, either, as some suppose, in one of the golden vessels connected therewith, or, more probably, by simply being spread out over the top of the loaves. Two things seem to have been represented by this part of our subject. When we see the white powder of the frankincense spread out all over the loaves upon the table, and when we bear in mind that those loaves were a figure of Christ, and that frankincense is a token of that which is pleasing, or grateful, *we seem to have exhibited, in beautiful symbol before us, the acceptableness of Christ and his work to the Father.* We are reminded of those different occasions, during the progress of our Saviour's personal ministry on earth, when the eternal Father, coming forth, as it were, from the awful majesty of His invisible throne, and pointing to the Incarnate Saviour, toiling onward in His painful path, proclaimed, with His own voice, the memorable words, " This is my beloved Son, in *whom I am well pleased.*" The golden table with its incense-covered bread was a pleasing object to the Father. His eye rested on it with delight, because it stood before Him as the significant symbol or representative of His Beloved Son. And so the preaching of the gospel, irrespective altogether of its saving influence on the souls of men, is declared to be "a sweet savor unto God." God is pleased with the exercise of the ministry in itself considered. The simple thing of holding forth "the truth as it is in Jesus" is that in which He delights. When Christ is lifted up, in the presence of ruined men, as the bread which came down from heaven, a service is rendered, in the highest sense acceptable to God. And this truth was symbolised, in the Jewish tabernacle, when the shew-bread was seen, standing on the golden table, covered all over with the white powder of the frankincense.

But, there is another thought suggested, and illustrated, by this part of our subject, and *that is the intercession of Christ as the procuring cause of all our spiritual enjoyments and blessings*. When the loaves were removed from the table, on the Sabbath, they were given to the officiating priests. They were to eat them, and none but they. And while they were doing this, the frankincense, which had lain scattered over the surface of the loaves, was collected into one of the golden vessels, and "burned by fire as an offering before the Lord." There are the priests satisfying their hunger with the bread which has been taken from the golden table, and deriving strength and comfort from it; and even while they are thus occupied, the incense is burning, and its fuming clouds are rising, with grateful fragrance, before the presence of the Lord. What a beautiful symbol this was of Christ's intercession, as connected with all our spiritual enjoyments, and the procuring cause of all our blessings! We read God's word, and are comforted by it; we bow in prayer before the mercy-seat and are refreshed; we gather round the sacramental board and find our souls "strengthened by the body and blood of Christ, as our bodies are by the bread and wine;" we listen to the preaching of the gospel; its doctrines distil as the dew upon our souls, making them to grow and flourish like a watered garden; but while we thus sit in heavenly places in Christ Jesus, and find ourselves abundantly satisfied with the plenteousness of His house, let us never, never forget the connection of all this circle of privilege with the gracious service of our Great High Priest within the veil. There the incense of His merits is diffusing its grateful fragrance unceasingly before the mercy-seat, and we are receiving the benefits of the same when the golden oil of His grace flows down to strengthen and comfort, to sanctify and save our souls.

Such are some of the lessons shadowed forth by the table of shew-bread, as it occupied its appointed place in the Jewish Tabernacle.

In conclusion, it seems like a natural inference from this subject to speak of the choice provision God has made for the spiritual sup-

ply of His people in the wilderness of this world. It was symbolised, in the tabernacle, by the bread upon the golden table. This indeed was for the priests only. But, under the gospel dispensation, we know, *all* the Lord's people are priests. They are all permitted to enter the sanctuary and eat of that which this shew-bread represented. The bread of the tabernacle was choice bread. It was made of the finest wheat. It might well be called " bread from heaven." Now did it ever occur to you to ask the question where the flour came from of which this bread was made in the wilderness ? Of course the wandering tribes could sow no seed, and reap no harvests on the burning sands of the desert. To carry grain or flour with them through the forty years of their sojourn was an absolute impossibility. The material then of which this bread was made must have been furnished by miracle. Nor is it surprising that this should have been so. When the table of the people was fed by miracle for six days in the week, it is hardly likely that the Lord's table, on the Sabbath, should have been supplied from a lower source. And this bread, of the finest wheat, thus miraculously provided, how striking a symbol it was of Christ, "the bread which came down from heaven," in the most true and literal sense. And it is on that the souls of His people live in this world. And this being the case, we cannot wonder to notice the strong expressions which God employs to characterize the spiritual provision made for His people in the sanctuary. In one place He calls it,—"marrow and fatness,"—Ps. lxiii. 5; in another it is—"wine and milk," Is. lv. 1.; in another it is,—"honey out of the rock," Ps. lxxxi. 16; again it is, "a feast of fat things and wine on the lees, well refined,"

Is. xxv. 6; and yet again it is spoken of as "the corn of heaven and angel's food," Ps. lxxviii. 25. And there is really less of figure about these expressions than we ordinarily suppose. For "the truth as it is in Jesus" is literally "angels' food." They live on God. Their souls are enlightened, sustained, and blessed by the truth that relates to the character of God. But of this we have no reason to suppose that the angels know anything except as it is revealed to them through Christ. And thus it is true that angels in heaven, as well as saints on earth, live on Him. How exalted and glorious is the position of a Christian! He feeds on angels' food. He gathers clusters from the vines of the heavenly Canaan, even while wandering through the wilderness. He drinks from wells fed by that "river whose streams make glad the city of God." Who would not be a Christian! No wonder that David should esteem the fare of God's sanctuary, more than his necessary food; and speak of it as "sweeter than honey, and the honeycomb." And no wonder that Paul so exulted "in the excellency of the knowledge of Christ Jesus his Lord." Men of literature and science find pleasure in their chosen pursuits, and there is, unquestionably, much real enjoyment in them. But all the joy which the whole range of nature yields, compared to that which the believer finds in Jesus, is but as the husk, or the shell to the kernel. Follower of Christ, how satisfied, how cheerful you should be! How you should rejoice in your portion! "Happy are the people who are in such a case! Yea, blessed are the people who have the Lord for their God!"

And you, beloved hearers, who are not Christians, why stand you afar off from this blessedness? Apart from Jesus there is

THE TABLE OF SHEW-BREAD. 225

nothing in the universe that can satisfy the cravings of your deathless spirits. The pangs of eternal hunger must prey upon you if you feed not on this living bread. Oh, is there not provision made for you in the sanctuary?

> " Why are its bounties all in vain
> Before unwilling hearts displayed?
> Was not for *you* the victim slain?
> Are you denied the children's bread?"

" In our Father's house is bread enough, and to spare;" and you perish with hunger. Will you not arise and go to your Father, and say unto him, " Father, I have sinned against heaven, and in thy sight, and am no more worthy to be called thy son?" He will receive you and bless you. He will bring forth the best robe, even the garment of salvation, the robe of Jesus' righteousness, and put it on you. And then there will be "joy in the presence of the angels of God" over another sinner that repenteth. May God in mercy give the grace that will bring every wandering prodigal here present to-night thus home to his Father's house for Jesus' sake—AMEN!

CHAPTER VI.

The Altar of Incense.

"And thou shalt make an altar to burn incense upon: of shittim-wood shalt thou make it. A cubit shall be the length thereof, and a cubit the breadth thereof; four-square shall it be; and two cubits shall be the height thereof; the horns thereof shall be of the same. And thou shalt overlay it with pure gold, the top thereof, and the sides thereof round about, and the horns thereof; and thou shalt make unto it a crown of gold round about. And two golden rings shalt thou make to it under the crown of it, by the two corners thereof, upon the two sides of it shalt thou make it; and they shall be for places for the staves to bear it withal. And thou shalt make the staves of shittim-wood, and overlay them with gold. And thou shalt put it before the vail that is by the ark of the testimony, before the mercy-seat that is over the testimony, where I will meet with thee. And Aaron shall burn thereon sweet incense every morning: when he dresseth the lamps, he shall burn incense upon it. And when Aaron lighteth the lamps at even, he shall burn incense upon it; a perpetual incense before the Lord throughout your generation. Ye shall offer no strange incense thereon, nor burnt sacrifice, nor meat offering; neither shall ye pour drink offering thereon."—EXODUS, xxx. 1—9.

VI.

There was something very interesting and striking in the nature of the miracle by which the prophet Elijah was sustained, while he was an inmate of the lowly dwelling of the widow of Sarepta. It was a time of famine. When he came to the home of that poor woman, her sole supply, for herself and child, consisted of a handful of meal at the bottom of a barrel, and of a little oil in a cruse. She was about to make what she supposed would be her *last* cake, that she and her child might eat it and die. Yet she believed the prophet's word when he assured her, in the name of God, of a miraculous supply during all the days of the famine. She acted in accordance with this faith, and the prophet's word was verified. For through all the years of the famine "the barrel of meal wasted not, neither did the cruse of oil fail." We marvel at this, whenever we reflect upon it. And yet we have something analogous to it in God's dealing with his Church. Look at this bible. It is a little volume which you can carry in your pocket. It contains some chapters of history, a little poetry, some prophecy, a few biographical sketches, and several letters. This is all. You can teach the substance of its contents to your child before he leaves the nursery. How like the widow's handful of meal in the barrel this is! And yet, *this* is *all* the household of God have to live upon spiritually. Yes, and it is all they *need* to have. They never can get through with it. For long centuries they have lived upon it. Yet still, from age

THE ALTAR OF INCENSE. 231

to age, the truth remains—the miracle continues—and "the barrel of meal wasteth not, neither does the cruse of oil fail."

The exhaustlessness of scripture! how often, as we handle it, we are impressed, and almost overpowered with this thought! This train of thought is suggested by the simplicity and plainness of the object we are now to consider, and yet the fulness of the instruction imparted by it.

Our present subject is—*The altar of incense and the lessons which it teaches.*

There were two altars connected with the Jewish Tabernacle; one of these was of brass, the other of gold. The former stood without, in the court of the tabernacle, the latter stood within the tabernacle, in the Holy Place. The former was connected with the shedding of blood, and the offering of animal sacrifices; the latter was connected with the burning of sweet spices, and the rising thence of clouds of fragrant incense. The truths that centred in the one told of the atonement offered for the sins of God's people; the fuming incense offered on the other told of the high calling of God's people, and the acceptableness of their persons and services in His sight. But though representing aspects of truth widely different in their character, yet these two altars were most intimately and indissolubly related to each other. The golden altar owed all the utility and worth of its service to the sprinkling upon it of the blood that had been shed upon the brazen altar; and the fire which caused the incense to send forth its clouds of fragrant smoke from the altar in the Holy Place was kindled from the coals which had consumed the victim on the altar of burnt-offering.

This golden altar constituted the third article of the furniture of the Holy Place.

As the priest entered the sanctuary from the outer court, it stood directly in front of him, at an equal distance from the candlestick and the table of shew-bread, and immediately in front of the vail, or curtain which separated the Holy Place from the Most Holy.

The materials of which this altar was composed, like those of the ark itself, and most other parts of the sacred structure, were the shittim, or acacia wood overlaid with gold.

The dimensions of this altar are given with great distinctness and precision. Its height was two cubits, or three feet of our measure. In length and breadth the sides were one cubit, or 18 inches each. The height of this golden altar exceeded that of any other article of the tabernacle furniture whose dimensions are given by the sacred writer. The dimensions of the candlestick are not stated. But the golden altar was higher by half a cubit than either the table of shew-bread, or the ark of the covenant. Thus it took the lead in the tabernacle; its summit rose more to a level with Him whose dwelling place was "between the Cherubim over the mercy-seat," and thence was wafted the fragrant cloud, which sheltered under its perfume both the priest who ministered, and the other vessels of the sanctuary. This teaches us the lofty standing of our Great High Priest in the sanctuary above. His first entrance there, clothed in the garment of our humanity, added a new and sweet odor to the heavenly temple. A cloud of human fragrance rolled up, mingling itself with the cloud of divine glory, and the dwelling place of the Most High was filled with the holy perfume. It covers over every ill-savor that otherwise might be wafted from the worshipper on earth in the Holy

Place. It presents its fragrance immediately "before the Lord," so that no weakness, no failure on the part of His people, may hinder their ready access to the throne of grace.

This altar was furnished with horns, or projections at the several corners, though the purpose for which they were intended does not appear.

Like the table of shew-bread, the altar of of incense had "a crown of gold round about." This denoted here, as in the former case, a rim, or border, by which the censor, containing the coals of fire which consumed the incense, would be preserved in its place.

There was a ring on each of the opposite corners of the altar, directly under the crown, or rim, through which staves were placed for the purpose of carrying it about, in the journeyings of the people through the wilderness.

Let this suffice for the description of the golden altar. We proceed now to notice the practical lessons taught us by this article of the tabernacle furniture.

We gather our first lesson from THE SHAPE AND POSITION OF THIS ALTAR.

The altar was four-square. Its length and its breadth were equal. A square is a compact, even-sided figure, and it seems to have been especially chosen for the form of the altar as if to represent the completeness and fulness of the work effected thereon, whether of sacrifice or of incense. The same measure and estimate were thus presented every way, whether towards God, or towards man. But the squareness of the altar also denoted the firmness and stability of the service connected with it. Prayer and praise are not temporary things. They were not designed to abide merely while *that* dispensation lasted, or *this* with which we stand connected. *Prayer* indeed will be confined to earth, for it is the language of want, the outgoing of desire unsatisfied. But "praise waiteth for God" in the heavenly, as well as in the earthly Zion. It is the company of the redeemed, in the glory of their everlasting state that our Divine Saviour has in view when He says,—" In the midst of the Church will I sing praise unto Thee." Ps. xxii. 22. And David expresses the same idea, in the words so beautifully rendered in our metrical version :—

> " I'll praise my Maker with my breath;
> And when my voice is lost in death
> Praise shall employ my nobler powers:
> My days of praise shall ne'er be past,
> While life and thought, and being last,
> And immortality endures."

The golden altar stood, as we have seen, in front of the vail, or directly before the mercy-seat. There was no possible way of approach to the ark of the covenant, and the mercy-seat upon it, but by this altar. And as this altar, with the incense burning upon it, points to Christ and the merits of his sacrifice, we cannot look upon it, in the position it occupies, without seeing in it a most beautiful and impressive illustration of the solemn truth announced by our Saviour when he said,—" No man cometh unto the Father but by me." As we thus gaze upon this golden altar, it is as though each of its four horns were pointing to Christ, while upon its glittering, blood-sprinkled sides we seem to see inscribed the lines of the hymn we often sing—

> " *Thou* art the way, to Thee alone,
> From sin and death we flee,
> And he who would the Father seek,
> Must seek Him Lord by Thee."

But see now how this altar stands. In properly arranged diagrams, or drawings,

THE ALTAR OF INCENSE.

it is represented as standing cornerwise, having an angle, and consequently a horn, turned toward the spectator instead of a full, square side. This position has been adopted from the consideration of the fourth verse of the passage chosen for our present text. Here we read, "And two golden rings shalt thou make to it, under the crown of it, by the two corners thereof, upon the two sides of it shalt thou make them; and they shall be for places for the staves to bear it withal." From this it is plain that there were but two rings for these staves, and not four; and that these rings were placed at two opposite corners immediately under the crown. This would render it necessary that the altar should be carried *cornerwise*, rather than in what we should term a *square* position. And as it was carried, so it would be deposited, and so it would stand in the tabernacle. The object of this variation from all the other vessels of the tabernacle which had staves,—each of the others having four rings—was, it is believed, in order that one of the horns of the altar should be directed toward each part of Israel's host. The tabernacle itself stood east and west; and the four camps of Israel took up their positions, severally, with reference to this holy dwelling; Judah, east; Reuben, south; Ephraim, west; and Dan, north. If the altar stood, as we are supposing, angularly in the Holy Place, one of its horns would then be pointing to each of these four camps; and the incense from its summit would have equal reference, in all its power and value, to each portion of God's chosen family. Does not this afford us a beautiful type of the intercession of Christ, offered alike, in all its efficacy and fragrance, for every portion of his people? How delightful to think of the savor of that sweet perfume as ascending with reference to north, south, east, and west; and of its efficiency and fulness as presented alike in behalf of every believing soul! Now, that the people of God are scattered to the four winds of heaven, separated from one another, and broken up into little fragments, how comforting it is to remember that all are presented by Christ in unbroken unity, and in full perfectness before God!

But then, there is another truth taught us by these horns of the golden altar. Observe their pointing was *only* to the *tribes of Israel.* The service with which they stood connected, and all the blessings following in its train, constituted part of the privilege peculiar to the family of God. It was a privilege restricted to them. And this is equally true of the intercession of Christ, typified by the golden altar and its incense. This intercession, in its saving influence, at least, is restricted to the members of His own family. I have spoken on former occasions of the atonement of Christ as unlimited in its nature. This language was only intended to apply to the *worth*, or *merits* of His sacrifice. In that respect, it was doubtless, in the beautiful language of the Prayer Book, "a full, perfect, and sufficient sacrifice for the sins of the whole world." But when you come to the *application* of the atonement, of course it is limited. And that which determines these limits is the absolute sovereignty of God. And so the intercession of Christ is limited. By his own teaching, He put an end to all real ground for controversy on this point, among those who desire simply to follow his guidance. What this is we see clearly in the words of the great prayer, which He offered in the night in which he was betrayed. Then, taking in His comprehensive grasp, all whom the Father had given to him—even all who should believe on Him down to the end of time, He says: "I *pray* for *them.*' And then, as if to guard against the possibility of misunderstanding His meaning, He puts in a negative form what He has just declared so positively, and affirms in the most emphatic and unqualified manner, the solemn, awful truth—"I *pray not for the world!*" The horns of the golden altar pointed to *all* the Israel of God—but *not* to others.

Our second lesson from the golden altar is taught us by THE CONDITION NECESSARY TO THE OFFERING OF ITS INCENSE, *viz., that there be a fire burning on it.*

The incense on this altar may be regarded as representing two things—viz., *the intercession of Christ, or the prayers of His people,* and our lesson here will be twofold as embracing both these ideas.

This incense on the altar typified the intercession of Christ. But the fragrance of the incense could not be brought out, nor its efficacy put forth *till the action of fire was employed.* And these burning coals on the golden altar, to what do they point us in this view of our subject but the sufferings of Christ? " It *behoved* Christ to suffer." It was His sufferings in the garden, on the cross, and all through the amazing scenes of His humiliation which gave worth to His atonement and efficacy to His intercession. These are the live coals which cause the incense of his merits to exhale its rich fragrance. It is when bruised and crushed that spices give forth their most delightful perfumes. The substances which made up the incense employed in the tabernacle had to be reduced to powder before it could be made use of. And so Christ was "wounded for our transgressions, and bruised for

THE ALTAR OF INCENSE. 245

our iniquities, and by his stripes we are healed." As the "captain of our salvation," He "was made perfect;" *i. e.*, fully prepared for all the duties of His exalted position, "through suffering." As God's own chosen lamb He was bound a bleeding victim on the brazen altar to be consumed by the fire of divine justice, before, as our great High-priest, He could take his stand beside the golden altar, or enter the presence of the Father, in the Holy Place not made with hands, bearing with him the fragrant incense of His own merits. This incense, on which our whole acceptance with God depends, would never have exhaled its fragrance, so grateful to the offended majesty of heaven, if it had not been consumed upon the burning coals of divine justice. This truth we are taught as we stand beside the golden altar and perceive the sweet savor diffused through the tabernacle as the priest scatters the incense on the fire burning there.

But we have another lesson taught us here. The golden censer, on this altar, with the incense rising from it, *denotes, we know, the prayers of God's people.* This St. John teaches us in one of his apocalyptic visions. Rev. viii. 3, 4. Here we read:—
"And another angel came and stood at the altar, having a golden censer; and there was given him much incense that he should offer it with the prayers of all the saints upon the golden altar which was before the throne. And the smoke of the incense, which came with the prayers of the saints, ascended up before God out of the angel's hand." Here again we see that *the incense could yield no fragrance without fire.* The priest put it on the *live coals*, and then the odorous clouds went fuming up, a sweet savor, acceptable to God. And here we are taught, in a most

significant way, the necessity of heartiness, or fervor in our worship, if we would have it well-pleasing to God. There must be the warmth of real affection, the fire of glowing love on the altar of our hearts, or there will be no fragrant incense going up with our prayers and praises. It was when his people had become cold and dead, and their religion had degenerated into a mere formal service; in other words, it was when the fire had gone out upon the golden altar, that God said to them, by the prophet: " Bring no more *vain oblations; incense* is an *abomination* unto me." Isaiah i. 13. How impressive the lesson here taught us of God's intense dislike of cold and formal worship, when we find Him calling the very offerings He had Himself ordained, " *vain oblations ;*" and the incense He had commanded, " *an abomination* " before Him, because it was not accompanied by the fire of sincere affection!

This is quite in keeping with the strong language applied by Him to the Laodicean Church, when He says: "I would thou wert cold, or hot; so, then, because thou art lukewarm, and neither cold nor hot, I will spue thee out of my mouth." Rev. iii. 15, 16. Nor can we be surprised at this, if we reflect that, as ransomed sinners, when we come before God in worship, we are surrounded by all the marvels and wonders of redeeming love. The thought of this "scale of miracles" should indeed "make every bosom burn, and every heart to bound."

"On such a theme 'tis impious to be cold:
　Passion is reason, transport temper here.
　Shall Heaven which gave us ardor, and has shown
　Her own for man so strongly, not disdain
　That prose of piety, a lukewarm praise?
　Rise odors sweet from incense uninflamed?
　Devotion when lukewarm is *un*devout;
　But when it glows its heat is struck to heaven;
　To human hearts her golden harps are strung;
　And Heaven's orchestra chants Amen to man.

Praise ardent, cordial, constant is to God
More fragrant than Arabia sacrificed,
And all her spicy mountains in a flame."

Our third lesson from this altar is taught us by the CONTINUOUSNESS OF THE INCENSE *upon it.*

We read in the seventh verse of the passage which constitutes our text—"And Aaron shall burn thereon sweet incense every morning: when he dresseth the lamps he shall burn incense upon it. And when he lighteth the lamps at even, he shall burn incense upon it, a perpetual incense before the Lord throughout your generations." The morning supply, it is supposed, lasted until evening; and the evening supply until the morning. Even in their journeying through the wilderness this service was kept up, and wherever their weary tribes were led, the sweet savor of this incense was going up before God, as a memorial in their behalf continually. Thus it was emphatically, as God designed it to be, "a *perpetual* incense."

How beautifully this points us to Jesus! His offering, once made upon the brazen altar, was never repeated; and so the incense of his merits, once thrown upon the fire on the golden altar, never needs to be repeated. The fire upon this altar never goes out, and the fragrance given forth from it never ceases to ascend. The intercession of Christ is uninterrupted. "He *ever liveth* to make intercession for us." "He does not plead for His people," says an English writer, "at distant intervals, forgetting them in the meanwhile, but is ever, at all times presenting their wants and trials before his Father. His intercession is not so much a succession of requests, as a constant stream of advocacy, at once ever varying with the varying circumstances of his people, and under all circumstances never ceasing."

"The high-priest of the earthly tabernacle went into the Holy of Holies, and appeared before the mercy-seat as the advocate of the people only once a year. At other times no voice was heard, no blood was sprinkled within that Most Holy Place, and from one day of atonement to another the Israelite was left without his intercessor."

"But it is not so with the High-priest of the heavenly sanctuary. Christ does not cast an occasional glance at our concerns, and then turn his attention to something more important. No, but in his Infinite mind, He embraces at once, all the necessities of his people, and while ruling all worlds, leaves not a moment of time unoccupied with thoughts for our good."

"He does this for all His people. There is not one of His believing children, for whom Jesus intercedes not, and for whom He is not interceding constantly. *Our* joys and hopes are passing and changeful; our prayers and praises vary with every wind of temptation, and are often drowned amid the roaring noise of the waves of this troublesome world; but the voice of our Intercessor is ever the same. We hear it not, but in heaven it sounds so earnestly as to stay the uplifted arm of Justice ere it fall; so sweetly as to make angels sometimes drop their harps to listen to it, and so constantly as never to leave one silent interval. The intercession of the Jewish high-priest was not merely occasional, while ours is constant; but that was only *temporary* while ours is *everlasting*. The tabernacle of Shiloh was removed. The temple at Jerusalem was destroyed. With it passed away the Mosaic ritual, and from that time no high-priest, except our great High-priest, has ever interceded for God's children. The Jewish high-priests are gone, but the Christian High-priest has an unchangeable priesthood. His existence and his priesthood are alike eternal; and therefore, Jesus, who interceded for his people in the time of the apostles, and obtained for them the outpouring of the Spirit, intercedes as really for us now, and will intercede for his saved people throughout eternity. Our deliverance from sin will not set us free from wants. On the contrary, every increase of happiness will hereafter, as well as now, bring with it an increase of necessities. The blessedness of heaven does not consist in having no wants, in being independent of God—but in having every want supplied. Even in heaven we shall need, and have our Intercessor. Through endless ages He will form a mirror, reflecting in His Father's sight all the wishes of the saints in glory, and giving back to them the bright rays of the Father's love. "This priest, because He continueth forever, hath an unchangeable priesthood. Wherefore He is able to save them to the uttermost that come unto God by Him, seeing He ever liveth to make intercession for them." (Garratt's Scripture Symbolism.)

Our fourth lesson from this subject is furnished by observing THE CONNECTION OF THE ALTAR OF INCENSE WITH BOTH THE OUTER AND THE INNER SANCTUARY.

The golden altar stood, as we have seen, in the outer sanctuary, the Holy Place, just before the vail. It was part of the furniture of the Holy Place. It *belonged* to that. The other articles of furniture in that place were hallowed by the odor of its incense. All the services performed there were perfumed by its fragrance, and thus rendered acceptable to God.

But on the great day of atonement, when

THE ALTAR OF INCENSE. 255

the high-priest entered through the vail into the Most Holy Place, he carried with him the censer, with its fuming incense, from off the golden altar. The inner, as well as the outer part of the sanctuary was pervaded by the fragrance of the same incense. All the service rendered in the one, as well as in the other, stood upon the same ground, was accepted on the same principle, and perfumed with the odor of the same sweet smelling savor.

Now we know that the outer part of the sanctuary, or the Holy Place, represented the Church on earth; while the inner part, or the Most Holy Place, represented the Church in heaven. The lesson taught us by the part of the subject now before us is, that the golden altar, with its incense, belongs alike to both these departments of the Church of Christ. All the service performed, and all the joy experienced by the redeemed in the Church on earth is based upon the sacrifice of Christ, and connected with the incense of his merits. And the same will be true of the redeemed in the Church in heaven. How sweet and precious is the thought of this point of practical connection between the Church in its militant and its triumphant state. We glory in the cross of Christ, here on earth. Our sweetest pleasures, our highest joys, are realized in connection with it.

> "Here it is we find our heaven,
>   While upon the Lamb we gaze;
> Here we see our sins forgiven,
>   Lost in wonder, love and praise."

And no view that could be given of the grandeur, or the glory of heaven, would be satisfying to the souls of the redeemed unless it taught them to associate with all the sources of their most ecstatic bliss the thought of intimate fellowship, and indissoluble connection with Jesus, the object of their supremest love. But we *are* taught this most clearly when we gaze upon the inner shrine of the tabernacle, and see *that*, as well as the outer division of it, pervaded by the clouds of incense from the golden altar. Whatever service we may be permitted to render, in the heavenly state, will be service rendered through Christ. Whatever glory we may attain to, or whatever happiness we may possess there, will still be glory and happiness, emanating from Christ and shared in connection with Him. And when in one place we hear Jesus thus praying for His people :—"Father, I will that they also whom thou hast given me, be with me, where I am ;"—when in another place we read of the redeemed standing before the throne arrayed in robes "washed and made white in the blood of the Lamb ;" when in another place we hear the anthem of accomplished redemption pealing through the arches of the upper sanctuary, and find that the ever-recurring chorus is—"Worthy is the Lamb that was slain to receive power, and riches, and wisdom, and strength, and honor, and glory, and blessing;" and when in another place we see the company of the ransomed in their homes of bliss, and hear Jesus say of them—"they shall walk *with me* in white, for they are worthy," or find it promised elsewhere, "the Lamb that is in the midst of the throne shall feed them, and lead them to fountains of living waters," *then* we are perfectly assured of the precious truth,—

> "Once in Christ, in Christ forever,
> So the unfailing word declares,
> Neither sin, nor death shall sever
> Jesus from his chosen heirs."

What a beautiful illustration we have here of the words of the apostle when he de-

THE ALTAR OF INCENSE. 259

clares that,—"Neither life nor death, nor angels, nor principalities, nor powers, nor things present, *nor things to come*, shall separate us from the love of God which is in Christ Jesus, our Lord." Rom. viii. 39.

And when we look upon the Jewish tabernacle and see the high-priest, all the while that he officiated in the Most Holy Place, covered with the cloud of incense, we are taught, by this significant shadow, that in all the glory and blessedness of the heavenly state the redeemed will ever be associated with Christ and dependent on Him.

Our fifth and last lesson from this subject is gathered from THE NATURE AND COMPOSITION OF THE INCENSE *offered upon the golden altar.*

We have a description of it given in the chapter from which our text is taken, Exod. xxx. 34—38. "And the Lord said unto Moses, take unto thee sweet spices, stacte, and onycha, and galbanum; these sweet spices, with pure frankincense: of each shall there be a like weight; and thou shalt make it a perfume, a confection after the art of the apothecary, tempered together, pure and holy; and thou shalt beat some of it very small, and put of it before the testimony in the tabernacle of the congregation, where I will meet with thee: it shall be unto you most holy. And as for the perfume which thou shalt make, ye shall not make to yourselves according to the composition thereof: it shall be unto thee holy for the Lord. Whosoever shall make like unto that, to smell thereto, shall even be cut off from his people."

Of course this points directly to Christ in his intercessory work. Now, observe this incense was composed of four substances. Three of these, onycha, stacte, and galbanum, were substances entirely unknown to

THE ALTAR OF INCENSE. 261

us. They lie outside of the circle of our knowledge. These may very well be regarded as pointing to the divinity of Christ, in the mysteriousness of its connection with His death and sacrifice. These are matters of which, like the three elements of the incense under consideration, we know nothing at all. They are mysteries to us. We know the facts connected with them, mentioned in the scriptures, as we know the names of these strange substances, but we know nothing more.

The frankincense was a substance with which we are acquainted. It was, we know, an aromatic, odoriferous gum, obtained by incisions from the bark of a tree named by the ancients Thurifera. This tree grows in Arabia, and around Mount Lebanon, and its leaves are said to resemble those of a pear-tree. We may regard this frankincense as representing the humanity of Christ. This we know and understand, for it was like our own, in all respects, save that it was free from sin.

The elements composing this incense were mingled together in equal parts. This seems to point significantly to the entire and perfect *harmony of character* which distinguished our glorious Saviour. There was nothing out of place in him. All the elements of his being were in full development, and beautiful, harmonious proportion. His people, for the most part, attain to eminence by the preponderance of some one element of character over others. Abraham was distinguished for his faith—Job for his patience, Moses for his meekness, David for his devotion, Elijah for his courage, Daniel for his wisdom, Peter for his impetuous ardor, and John for the loving gentleness of his spirit. But it was very different with Jesus. We see in Him, not single points of excellence, or features of character in partial development, but a full-orbed circle of loveliness, including every possible grace illustrated and combined in absolute perfection. In contemplating his character you may go round the entire circle of moral and spiritual excellence, and from whatever point of view you regard him, you are constrained to say of him, in all sincerity and truth, that he is "the chief among ten thousand, and altogether lovely."

Again, the materials of which the incense was composed had to be beaten into small particles, or reduced to powder before it was prepared to give out its rich fragrance. And so Jesus, our glorious Saviour, had to be brought very low, and stoop to the most wondrous humiliation before the golden censer of His merits could yield those sweet odors which are so refreshing to the souls of his people, and at the same time so well pleasing to God, and so efficacious to secure our acceptance before Him. How perfectly amazing to contemplate was the depth of Christ's humiliation! From the lofty heights of essential deity down to the low level of a ruined and dishonored humanity, what a descent! For "the brightness of the Father's glory, and the express image of His person" to be "found in fashion as a man," even in the "form of a servant," what condescension! Behold Him who made the world and everything in it; who gave to its inhabitants "life, and breath, and all things," become Himself a dweller in the world He had made! See! "He comes to his own, and his own receive Him not." He lives on unknown, rejected, despised. He is hungry and thirsty, and weary; dependent for his daily bread upon the alms of others. He is esteemed "a worm, and no man, the very scorn of men, and a by-word among the

THE ALTAR OF INCENSE. 265

people." His name is cast out as evil. He is reckoned a base fellow, "a ring-leader of sedition," a Samaritan, and a devil. He is classed with malefactors and murderers. He is "made a curse for us as He hung upon the tree." Ah! *this* was the process by which He who constitutes our incense was beaten fine, was ground to a powder that He might give forth an atoning, satisfying odor, whose fragrance should endure unwasted through eternity, and whose efficacy should prevail for every necessity of the uncounted multitude of His chosen people.

Such are the lessons we gather from the golden altar.

In conclusion, *we see from this subject the ground of the Christian's comfort in serving God.*

He knows that Jesus is always interceding for him before God. If you are a believer, God never beholds you but through the medium of the cloud of fragrant incense that rises unceasingly before Him from the golden censer of the merits of His own beloved Son. This cloud of incense is surrounding your person at all times. This is the point of view from which to see, in its true meaning, that passage which sets forth so sweetly the preciousness of the covenant relation in which God's people stand, when we are assured that "He doth not behold iniquity in Jacob, neither doth He see perverseness in Israel." Numb. xxiii. 21. When your prayers or praises are offered before God, though utterly unworthy, in themselves considered, of His notice or regard, yet the fragrance of this incense goes up with them, and secures their acceptance. When you perform any service for God, though it be the very best and holiest you can render, you know it to be marred with many short-comings, and stained with many imperfections; but when it is perfumed with the merits of the Great Mediator, it becomes at once a sweet savor, acceptable unto God. Wherever you go this incense accompanies you. Wherever you abide it abides with you. In lying down and rising up, in going out and coming in, in praying, and in praising, in acting and in suffering, in health and in sickness, in life and in death, in time and in eternity, the fragrance of this divine incense surrounds you. It fills the circle in which you live and move. It prevents and follows, pervades, and sanctifies every act you perform. Believer in Jesus! *this* is the relation in which you stand to the Lord God Almighty. Glorious privilege of the child of God! Who would not be a Christian?

But this subject also presents in a startling light the position and conduct of those who are not Christians.

For observe now, that on the authority of God's most positive and explicit declaration, the people were forbidden to use any other incense than that which He had provided. The prohibition ran thus: "And as for the perfume which thou shalt make, ye shalt not make to yourselves according to the composition thereof. Whosoever shall make the like unto it, shall even be cut off from his people." Exod. xxx., 37, 38. There is something very solemn in this prohibition. It seems like the great standing law of Jehovah, written with His own finger over this heaven-devised incense—"*To counterfeit is death!*" The soul that attempts to do this shall be cut off from his people. This is solemnly significant. It bears with tremendous power on all who have no saving interest in Christ. My dear hearer, not a Christian, on what are you depending for salvation? Is it your morality? Is it your alms-giving? Is it your Church connection? Is it the general idea of God's mercy? See what you are doing in clinging to any such hope; you are coming before God with other incense than that which He has ordained. You are counterfeiting that which He has marked as genuine. The very plea to which you are trusting will cover you with confusion, and pluck down heavier ruin on your head. Soul out of Jesus, you are undone. But seek an interest in Him, and then you will have part in his intercession—and the fragrant incense of his merits will be thrown around you, and rise up with acceptance before God in your behalf.

CHAPTER VII.

The Ark.

"And they shall make an ark of shittim-wood; two cubits and a half shall be the length thereof, and a cubit and a half the breadth thereof, and a cubit and a half the height thereof. And thou shalt overlay it with pure gold: within and without shalt thou overlay it; and shalt make upon it a crown of gold round about. And thou shalt cast four rings of gold for it, and put them in the four corners thereof; and two rings shall be in the one side of it, and two rings in the other side of it. And thou shalt make staves of shittim-wood, and overlay them with gold. And thou shalt put the staves into the rings by the sides of the ark, that the ark may be borne with them. The staves shall be in the rings of the ark; they shall not be taken from it. And thou shalt put into the ark the testimony which I shall give thee. And thou shalt make a mercy-seat of pure gold: two cubits and a half shall be the length thereof, and a cubit and a half the breadth thereof. And thou shalt make two cherubims of gold, of beaten work shalt thou make them, in the two ends of the mercy-seat. And make one cherub on the one end, and the other cherub on the other end; even of the mercy-seat shall ye make the cherubims on the two ends thereof. And the cherubims shall stretch forth their wings on high, covering the mercy-seat with their wings, and their faces shall look one to another; toward the mercy-seat shall the faces of the cherubims be. And thou shalt put the mercy-seat above upon the ark; and in the ark thou shalt put the testimony that I shall give thee. And there I will meet with thee, and I will commune with thee from above the mercy-seat, from between the two cherubims which are upon the ark of the testimony, of all things which I will give thee in commandment unto the children of Israel."—EXODUS, xxv. 10—22.

VII.

The scene of our last three sermons has lain within the precincts of the first division of the tabernacle. We have been meditating within the Holy Place. The candlestick, the table of shew-bread, and the golden altar of incense, have engaged our attention. These were all the articles of furniture contained in that portion of the sanctuary. We have concluded our examination of this part of the sacred structure. We are now to pass through that dark, mysterious veil,—to enter the Most Holy Place —to gaze in awe-inspiring meditation on the ark of the covenant, with the cloud of glory, the Shechinah, the awful symbol of the divine presence overshadowing it. It becomes us to approach it with reverence. The most sacred material object ever framed by the hand of man is to engage our attention. We seem to hear the voice of God addressed to each of us, saying, as it did to Moses at the bush—"Put off thy shoes from off thy feet, for the place whereon thou standest is holy ground."

Before entering the Most Holy Place, however, to examine the ark in detail, let us just glance at the position it occupied in the camp of Israel, both when the camp was at rest, and when in motion. The appearance of the camp at rest we considered in our opening discourse. That encampment constituted an oblong square, extending, probably, twelve miles on each side. The tabernacle was set up in the centre of this encampment, and the ark constituted the

THE ARK. 275

great central object of interest and attraction in the tabernacle.

But when the cloud moved from over the ark, giving the silent order of march, the aspect of things was entirely changed. The camp in motion presented a very striking contrast to the camp at rest. Let us suppose that this silent order has been given. The tabernacle is taken down. Its different parts are covered up, put in marching condition, and assigned to the different branches of the family of Aaron charged with the care of them. Then the line of march is taken in the following order: First, in solemn silence, the mysterious cloud goes before them to point out the way. Then Judah leads the van, followed by the tribes of Issachar and Zebulon, making an army of more than 180,000. Immediately after these come six wagons, under the care of Gershon and Merari, the sons of Ithamar.

Two of these wagons contain the coverings of the tabernacle, and the curtains of the court that surrounds it. The other four contain the golden boards, the silver sockets, and golden pillars of the tabernacle, and the court attached to it. Then follow the tribes of Reuben, Simeon, and Gad, 150,000 strong. After these, borne upon the shoulders of the Kohathites, come all the sacred furniture of the tabernacle, in charge of six different companies. First is the ark; then the golden altar of incense; then the candlestick; then the table of shew-bread; then the laver and the smaller golden vessels, and lastly the brazen altar. You will observe that, when arranged for the march, these sacred articles were disposed in an order directly the reverse of that which they occupied when the camp was at rest. After these came the tribes of Ephraim, Benjamin, and Manassah, numbering upwards of

108,000 men. The rear guard of the host was formed by the tribes of Dan, Asher, and Naphtali, consisting of 157,000 men. This was the order uniformly observed in marching. The general position of the ark was in the centre of the advancing host. There were but two exceptions to this, throughout the whole course of their long pilgrimage. These exceptions are found at the commencement, and at the close of their wanderings. The first of these occurred when the nation began their march from Sinai. There we find Moses trying to persuade Hobab, his father-in-law, to go with them, and he urged his request by the plea that he knew the way through the wilderness, and "might be to them *instead of eyes*." Immediately after this we read that "the ark of the covenant of the Lord went before them to search out a resting place for them." Numb. x., 33. It would seem as if God had altered the usual order of march on this occasion, and had sent the ark in advance of the host on purpose to reprove Moses for his want of faith. What need was there of the eyes of Hobab, or any other created being, to spy out their way when God Himself was their Leader and Guide? And then again, at the close of their long wanderings, when Jordan was to be crossed, God sent the ark before them. It was at *its* approach that the overflowing waters of the river divided in the midst, and opened up a way for the ransomed of the Lord to pass over. And the ark remained in the bed of the stream till all the multitudes of the wandering tribes had crossed in safety, as if to show us, when Jordan is considered as a figure or type of death, that the time, the place, and all the circumstances of that event are controlled by the covenant of grace, of which this ark was the symbol.

And as we think of the ark, standing midway in the emptied channel of the river, holding in check the tumultuous, threatening floods, and securing the entire safety of the overpassing multitudes of God's people, we have before us a beautiful illustration of the Psalmist's words, when he declares—"Precious in the sight of the Lord, is the death of his saints."

But let us proceed with our subject. We are to pass within the veil, and meditate on the ark of the covenant, as it stands in the Most Holy Place, resplendent with the glory that shines upon it from the mysterious overshadowing Shechinah. And to take in the subject in all its bearings, our attention will be directed to six several points, only a part of which can engage our meditations on the present occasion. We shall consider in the *first place, the veil, by which the ark was hidden from view. Secondly, the place in which the ark stood, called the Most Holy Place. Thirdly, the structure of the ark. Fourthly, its contents. Fifthly, the cherubim which overshadowed it; and lastly, the mercy-seat, with its irradiating glory.*

We begin then by considering the veil by which the ark was hid, and which separated the Holy Place from the Most Holy.

A thick heavy veil of tapestry, beautifully wrought with flowers and cherubim, was that which shut in the ark, and divided the tabernacle into two parts. Blue, purple, and scarlet were the colors blended in this veil. Josephus says of it: "This veil was very ornamental, and embroidered with all sorts of flowers which the earth produces, and there was interwoven into it all sorts of variety that might be an ornament." This veil of the tabernacle was the same as that which subsequently hung in the temple, and was rent in twain when our Lord expired on the cross. We may look at it from two points of view, *considering what it symbolised when it was an unrent veil, and what the rending of it signifies.*

The unrent veil was a symbol of *darkness* and *difficulty*. To the Jew, it shut out his view of heavenly things, and obstructed his way of approach to them. That veil was a *concealing* thing. All that stood behind it was effectually hidden from sight. But that Most Holy Place represented heaven. And thus, by the unrent veil, as St. Paul says: " The Holy Ghost this signified, that the way into the holiest of all was not yet made manifest." Heb. ix., 8. Very little was known under the former dispensation of the things of the heavenly world. The veil which hung over them could not be penetrated. The children of God tried indeed to peer through its thick folds with the eye of faith, and catch feeble glimpses of what lay beyond. Nor were these efforts wholly unavailing. Enoch, in the far off darkness of antediluvian ages, had a view of Christ's second coming to judgment. Job knew that his Redeemer lived, and that in his flesh, a partaker of his nature, he should yet see God. Abraham, and the patriarchs, looked for a city that hath foundations, whose builder and maker is God." David trusted to his covenant God to guide and support him through the dark valley of the shadow of death, and show him the path of life. Thus these holy men of old had glimpses of heavenly things. Yet they were but dimly seen. They were emphatically "things within the veil." That unrent veil was a *darkening* thing. It was at the same time an *obstructing* thing. It barred the entrance to the heavenly place. The holiest and best of God's people could not pass within that veil. The High-priest alone might enter, and he but once a year. The people knew, as he disappeared from their sight, that he was before the ark, sprinkling the blood, and waving the incense, and presenting his prayers in their behalf. They knew that *his* eyes looked upon all the hallowed things that were there, but *they* could not enter in to see and to pray for themselves. When Adam was driven forth from Paradise we read that at the entrance to that happy place from which he was expelled, God caused to be placed—" Cherubim and a flaming sword, which turned every way to keep the way of the tree of life." And this idea is still kept up when we see that veil, covered over with figures of the cherubim, and hanging down before the Jew to warn him off from all approach to the great central source of life and light. Thus the unrent veil was a *darkening*, and an *obstructing* thing.

But what does the *rent* veil signify? of

course the opposite of that which the *un*rent veil represented. If the veil unrent was designed to cover, or hide, the rent veil is designed to disclose or reveal. If the one was a symbol of darkness, the other is the emblem of light. And Jesus, we know, came as "the light of the world." He is the revealer of secrets, the unraveller of mysteries. He "brought life and immortality to light by the gospel." He came to "tell us plainly of the Father." And *now*, his people have "an unction from the Holy One, and *know all things*." Through the rent veil of Christ's flesh the light and glory of the upper sanctuary shine forth, and "in His light they see light." Thus the rent veil proclaims to us that "the darkness is past, and the true light now shineth."

But then it also signifies the *removal of obstructions* as well as the dispelling of darkness. All hindrances are taken out of the way of access to the mercy-seat. There is no longer any covering veil, any interposing barrier. What none but the High-Priest could do, under the Jewish economy, *all* God's people may do now. And what even he could do but once a year, they may do at all times. They can "enter into the holiest by the blood of Jesus." The way to the mercy-seat lies open at all times, and "whosoever will" may come and find mercy and grace to help in time of need. But it is not only the way of access to the mercy-seat by faith now, which this rent veil indicates. It does more than that. "The veil is rent," says the eloquent Melville, "to show that the Mediator made a passage into heaven, but in nothing does He act for himself alone. We rose with him; we ascended with him; and therefore is the rending of the veil as much a pledge of our admission as of his, who, by the efficiency of his sacrifice, provided for our being not only sons of God, but joint heirs with himself. The veil is rent. Then, with it should be rent away all doubt, and all unbelief. The door of heaven, the way of access to God's *glorified* presence hereafter, as well as to his *gracious* presence now, is thrown open by the work of mediation. We may not only draw nigh to God now in prayer, but we shall draw nigh to Him hereafter in person. We shall rise from the dust; we shall tread the firmament; we shall enter by the gates of pearl, and we shall walk the streets of gold. Blessed be God for this rent veil! Like a window opened in the sky, there have come forth through it the shinings of eternity, the promises of immortality, rich and lively visions of the inheritance of the saints in light."

And these are the lessons we gather from the veil that hangs before the ark.

But now we pass within this veil, and *consider as our second point—the place in which the ark stood.*

How well may our spirits feel unwonted awe come over them, as we enter the hallowed precincts of this inner shrine of the sanctuary. In a higher sense than that in which Jacob used the language as he awoke from his dream, we may say in truth,—" *This* is none other than the house of God, and this is the gate of heaven !" Nay, not only the *gate* of heaven, but, as it were, heaven itself. This is the audience chamber of the King of kings. " He who inhabiteth eternity, and the praises thereof, whose name is holy," established his abode and manifested his presence here. This circumstance tended to make this department of the tabernacle the most solemn and sacred spot within the confines of our globe. And everything about it was in keeping with this character.

Look at its *form*. This was that of a cube. The exact dimensions of this part of the sanctuary are not given. But in the temple, which Solomon subsequently built, at Jerusalem, the Most Holy Place, as we are distinctly informed, was cubical in its form, being twenty cubits, or thirty feet in each direction—the height, and the length, and the breadth of it being equal. And as the temple, in its essential features, was fashioned after the tabernacle, so as to be conformed to "the pattern showed to Moses in the Mount," there can be no question but that the same proportion in regard to the dimensions of the Most Holy Place existed in them both. The dimensions of this part of the tabernacle were those of a cube. The measure of its sides, its ceiling, and its floor was all the same. The cube is the most perfect of all forms, the natural emblem of perfection. And it was very appropriate that this hallowed place,—the type, or emblem of heaven, should have this feature stamped upon it. And it is worthy of note that the city which the prophet Ezekiel saw in vision,—probably designed to represent the earthly Jerusalem, as it will exist in the Millennial and everlasting age of our world—was in the form of a cube. And the still more glorious city which St. John saw in the Apocalyptic vision, the New Jerusalem, the most finished and elaborate symbol of the heavenly state, which the scriptures furnish, was a city cubical in its form. " The length, and the breadth, and the heighth of it were equal."

And as the *form* of this place denoted its perfection, so did the *material* of which it was composed. Gold, pure gold was the material. This met the eye on every side. Gold is the purest and most precious of the metals. In its way, too, gold stands as the symbol of perfection. When we say of a thing that it reaches the *golden* stage, we say that which expresses the highest idea of its development. Human vocabularies have no stronger terms to furnish. Human experience or thought cannot carry us beyond this. And so this golden chamber of the tabernacle, as we gaze upon the radiance of its glittering walls, stands before us a silent, but most significant type of the perfection of that heavenly abode whose gates are pearl; whose streets are gold— yes, and that, too, *transparent* gold; whose streams are crystal, and whose foundations are of all manner of precious stones.

This beautiful apartment of the tabernacle, how apt an emblem it was of that heavenly Zion which is the perfection of beauty!

> "Beautiful Zion, built above!
> Beautiful city—home of love!

Beautiful gates of pearly white!
Beautiful temple, God its light!

Beautiful crowns on every brow!
Beautiful palms the conquerors show!
Beautiful robes the ransomed wear!
Beautiful all who enter there!

Beautiful throne for God the Lamb!
Beautiful seats at God's right hand!
Beautiful rest! all wanderings cease!
Beautiful home of perfect peace!"

And then the *furniture* of this hallowed place spoke the same language. This told of perfection too. And what was this? One object alone met the eye here. This was that great central object of interest in this whole sacred structure,—that keystone of this arch,—that sun in the midst of this grand system,—that gem in the heaven-formed ring of these hallowed services,—*the ark of the covenant*. St. Paul indeed speaks of the "golden censer" as belonging to this Most Holy Place; and some have felt at a loss how to explain this, knowing as we do that the golden altar, with its incense, belonged clearly to the other division of the tabernacle. But there is really no difficulty in the case at all. The golden censer was not a part of the furniture of this portion of the sanctuary. Its appointed place was on the golden altar in the Holy Place. But when the High-priest, on the great day of atonement, made his annual visit within the veil, he carried the golden censer with him. Its fragrant perfume then pervaded every part of that most sacred spot, and rose up in graceful clouds before the ark. But on his return, he carried the censer with him. That was not its permanent place. *The ark alone was there.* Of the contents of the ark we shall speak in another place. There was nothing in the Most Holy Place but what was contained in the ark. How significant this was! The place we are considering denotes heaven. The ark which stands in it, as the sole object of interest and attraction there, is an emblem of Christ. And as there was nothing in the Most Holy Place but what was contained in the ark, so in heaven there is nothing on which the eye of the ransomed will rest, and nothing that their souls can need, but what is in Christ. The very radiance which lighted up this hallowed spot, and revealed its unearthly glories, was,— not the light of the sun, no, nor even the rays from the golden candlestick in the Holy Place—but that which was ever shining forth from the mysterious shechinah, that encircled and hovered over the ark. What a sweet shadowing forth of heavenly realities we have here! David was grasping the very substance of this precious truth when his loving heart went out in earnest longings after his Saviour God, as he asked—"Whom have I in heaven but Thee? and there is none upon earth that I desire in comparison with Thee." *"Complete in Him"* is what the ark, as the sole and all-comprehending object, existing in the Most Holy Place, proclaims, with silent eloquence, as the relation of the believing soul to Christ in heaven. The rest of heaven is rest in Christ. The righteousness of heaven is righteousness in Christ. The joy of heaven is joy in Christ. The light of heaven is light in Christ. Yea, says the apostle, as he gazes delightedly on the vision before him—"For the Lamb is the light thereof." The title to heaven is a title in Christ. The glory of heaven is glory in Christ. "Father, I will that they also whom thou hast given me be with me where I am, that they may behold my glory." What a precious, comprehensive, enduring truth the apostle declares when he affirms that "Christ is *all* and *in* all." Whether in the church below, or in the church above, it is a truth now, and will remain a truth forever, that "in Him all fulness dwells." The believing soul looks up to Jesus with adoring gratitude, and says:

> "Where'er *Thou* art is heaven to me,
> And heaven without Thee—cannot be!"

These are the precious thoughts suggested by the place in which the ark stood.

The third point we were to notice calls us to consider THE STRUCTURE OF THE ARK.

Like most of the other parts of the furniture of the tabernacle, the structure of the ark was plain and simple. It consisted merely of a square box or chest. Its length was two cubits and a half, or three feet eleven inches. Its breadth and height each one cubit and a half, or two feet seven inches. The materials of which it was composed, as with most of the other articles of the tabernacle furniture, were the shittim or acacia wood and gold. It was called "the ark of the covenant," or of the testimony, because it contained the law, written on tables of stone, which law was God's testimony to man, respecting his duty, and the keeping of which, on the part of Christ, became the ground of the covenant of grace to men. And for this reason Christ is said to be "given *for* a covenant of the people." The ark was hollow. The top, or lid that covered it was moveable. At each end were two rings, in which were inserted the staves by which it was carried. Around the top there was a rim or crown; and from the ends of it cherubim arose, whose outspread wings met, as if in overshadowing embrace, above the mercy seat.

This ark was a symbol of Christ. The constituent parts of it seemed to represent the two natures of our Saviour, The wood of the ark aptly emblemized the human nature of Christ. The tree from which this wood was obtained had its growth in the wilderness. And so in the development of his humanity, it was declared of Christ that " He should grow up like a root out of a dry ground." The acacia wood was incorruptible. It was not subject to decay. The ark which Moses built in the wilderness had lasted for a thousand years, before it was carried captive to Babylon, and it was then in a state of excellent preservation. And it is just so with the humanity of Christ. That humanity experienced no decay in life; it was the subject of none in death. He saw no corruption in the grave. He will see none forever. The humanity of Christ has now been for near 2,000 years seated at the right hand of the throne of God; the weight of universal government has rested on it; the radiance of heaven's glory has beamed around it, yet still its energy is undecayed, its beauty undiminished. And so it will remain through all the ages of eternity. Thus the wood of the ark represented the humanity of Christ.

And in like manner *the gold of the ark represented his divinity.* Gold is the most precious of all the metals; and so Christ is the most precious of all possible beings. Gold bears a high polish. It never rusts. It is the most beautiful, as well as the most precious of all the metals. And this is emphatically true of Christ. He is "the brightness of the Father's glory and the express image of his person." He is "the chief among ten thousand, and altogether lovely." And as these two substances, the wood and the gold, blended together to form the ark, so, in the language of our second article—these "two whole and perfect natures, that is to say, the Godhead and the manhood, were joined together in one person, never to be divided, whereof is one Christ, very God, and very man." He was " God manifest in the flesh." And as we trace the course of our blessed Lord from the manger to the cross, it is interesting to notice the many evidences that appear of the existence of these blended natures. It is the humanity that appears in the infant of a day lying in a manger. It is the divinity which is recognized in the attendant song of the angels, and in the adoring worship of the shepherds and the wise men. It was the humanity which appeared when Jesus submitted to receive the water of baptism from the hands of John the Baptist in the river Jordan. It was the divinity which was owned when the Spirit descended on him in the form of a dove, and the voice was heard from the throne of the Father, saying,—" This is my beloved Son, in whom

I am well pleased." The humanity was seen when he sat down, weary with toil, to rest himself by Jacob's well; the divinity displayed itself when he read and revealed the secret thoughts of the woman of Samaria, and by his mighty power made her, then and there, a child of God. The humanity was proved when, in crossing the sea of Galilee, he lay down in the hinder part of the ship, overpowered by his unceasing labors, and sank into unconscious slumber; the divinity shone forth, how gloriously! when he arose in all his majesty, and rebuked the winds and the sea, and immediately there was a great calm. The humanity of Jesus was attested when, as he hung upon the cross, he exclaimed, "I thirst;" but it was to his divinity that the dying thief appealed when he prayed—"Lord remember me when thou comest into thy kingdom;" and that divinity burst forth resplendently, like the sun from behind a dark cloud, when the expiring Saviour responded to that prayer, saying,— "To-day thou shalt be with me in Paradise." And as we gaze on these strange blendings of the human and the divine in Jesus, we are but beholding marvellous illustrations of what the structure of the ark sets before us, when we see the wood and the gold so mingled in its make.

The fourth and last division of our subject to which we shall now direct attention is THE CONTENTS OF THE ARK.

When St. Paul is speaking of these in Heb. ix. 4, he mentions in his catalogue of the things contained in the ark, "the golden pot that had manna, and Aaron's rod that budded, and the tables of the covenant." There is a discrepancy between this account and that found in I. Kings, viii. 9, and II. Chron. v. x. Here we are told distinctly that "there was nothing in the ark save the two tables of stone which Moses put there at Horeb." Here you perceive that the golden pot of manna, and Aaron's rod, that budded, are not mentioned among its contents. The question is, how are we to reconcile these two apparently conflicting statements? This is very easily done, simply, by considering the accounts as referring to two very different periods, in the history of the ark. St. Paul's account, in the Hebrews, describes the contents of the ark during the wanderings of the Israelites in the wilderness, or while the tabernacle was still existing. But the account of the ark in Kings and Chronicles speaks of its contents when the wilderness had been passed through, the promised land had been entered, and the temple had been built. Now the ark, in its journeyings through the wilderness, represents the state of the church in this present world. The ark at rest, in the temple at Jerusalem, represents the state of the Church in the glory of the heavenly world. It is very natural and suggestive then that there should have been a difference between the contents of the ark in these two stages of its history. In the wilderness, corresponding to the present condition of the Church in the world, the manna was absolutely necessary to the support and comfort of the people, and so were also the ministrations of an earthly priesthood of the order of Aaron. Hence the budded rod, which denoted that priesthood, and the golden pot of manna *were* in the ark then. But as the manna ceased when Canaan was entered,—so when heaven is reached, the state represented by the ark in the temple in Solomon's days, Christ will be Himself the only food, and the only priest his people will need. It is not surprising then to hear it said of the ark during the stage of its history which represents this state,—that "there was nothing in the ark save the two tables of stone which Moses put there at Horeb." While in the wilderness the several things mentioned by St. Paul were all there; in the days of Solomon the tables of stone on which the law was written were all that the ark contained. Whether the things withdrawn from the ark were removed by design, by negligence, or violence, is not a matter of much moment. The important thing is that they *were there* at one period of the history of the ark, while at another period they were *not* there.

The ark of the covenant contained at last only the two tables of the law. These were preserved in the ark. This was a very significant fact. It illustrates two important truths. It proclaims the *perfect righteousness* and the *absolute security* of the children of the covenant.

It shows the *perfect righteousness* of the believer. The whole law was in the ark. Those material tables, in the literal ark, point us to Christ. *He* is our ark. And the whole law is in his heart. It is written there. It has been kept by Him. He came to do this. He delighted to do it. He *did* do it. He "magnified the law and made it honorable." In all the length and breadth of its requirements He kept it. He "fulfilled all righteousness." It was a steady, uniform, unqualified obedience which He rendered. It reached up to the highest, and down to the lowest, and out to the extremest requirement of the law. It was an obedience which God weighed in the finely adjusted balances of the heavenly sanctuary and found *not* wanting, in any respect. God accepted it, and was well pleased with it. It vindicated his government; it honored his character; it was all that He desired.

And this is the righteousness in which the believer stands before God. This is imputed unto him. It is considered as his own. He is dealt with by God as he would be if he had wrought out this righteousness himself. And when we remember how the whole law was kept in the ark, we see significantly symbolized, in this aspect of it, the perfect righteousness of the children of the covenant.

But it also illustrated their *absolute security*. The tables of the law were broken in the hands of Moses, but kept in the hands of Christ. The security of the covenant of salvation, and of all who are embraced by it, depends on the keeping of the law. Not, bear in mind, on the keeping of the law by the children of the covenant; that is an absolute impossibility; but on the keeping of the law by their Head, and representative; by Christ, the messenger, the author,

THE ARK. 307

the finisher, the embodiment of the covenant. And this is not a thing *to be* done; it is a thing *already accomplished*. It has been fully wrought out. Jesus had *this* in his mind, among other things, when, as he hung expiring on the cross, He exclaimed,—"*It is finished.*" The thing is done. It never can be undone. The foundation, on which the covenant of salvation rests, has been laid broad, deep, and immovable in the obedience of Christ,—in the law as kept by Him. This covenant has been firmly based on that foundation. God has bound these two things together, and nothing can separate them. And this we see indicated by what is now before us. Those tables of the law, preserved unbroken in the ark of the covenant, are the emblem or pledge of the entire safety, the absolute security of the believing soul. Look at the position of the ark. It stood in the Most Holy Place,—

under the shadow of Jehovah's outspread wings—and surrounded by the radiance of his glory. His eye was ever watching over it. His omnipotent arm was ever stretched out for its defense. How perfectly safe it was! Child of the covenant, *this* is the type of your security in Jesus! It is perfect, absolute, inviolable security. And these are the thoughts suggested by the contents of the ark. Thus we have attempted to gather up the lessons taught us by the four several things connected with the ark that have now passed under our notice, viz.—*the veil that hung before the ark; the place in which the ark stood; the structure of the ark; and its contents.*

In conclusion—*How striking are some of the points of contrast between the Jewish and the Christian ark.* The one was composed of created materials. The time had been when the wood and the gold, wrought up into the form of the ark, had no existence. The other, as to the most important part of his being, at least, was constituted "from everlasting, from the beginning, or ever the world was." Travel, as far back as you will, over the trackless wastes of the eternity past, and you never can reach the point where you can plant yourself and say— " here, the divinity of Christ, the most important element in the constitution of our ark, was not in existence." The Jewish ark was prepared by *human* hands. The Christian ark was moulded and built by the hands of a *divine* Artificer. Hence we read that when the angel Gabriel announced to the Virgin Mary the birth of her wondrous child, he said,—" The Holy Ghost shall come upon thee, and the power of the Highest shall overshadow thee; therefore, also, that holy thing that shall be born of thee shall be called the Son of God." Mystery hangs over the origin of life, in all its developments, it was to be expected that this mystery should assume its darkest form over that development of life in which the divine allied itself to the human. And it was in reference to this very circumstance, that Jesus, anticipating his entrance into our world, said to the Father—" a body hast *Thou prepared me.*" It is true, even of us, that " we are fearfully and wonderfully made;" but it was incomparably more so of Christ. The Jewish ark was a beautiful object to contemplate, but its glory and its beauty were as nothing when contrasted with the excelling splendor of our wondrous ark. The Jewish ark led a migratory existence. It was now in one place, and now in another. It once fell into the hands of its enemies, and was led by them into captivity. It was carried in triumph into the temple of Dagon, treated with insult, and perhaps robbed of some of its treasured things. Very striking here is the contrast between the Jewish and the Christian ark. Christ, our ark, has abode in one place. His position is at the right hand of the majesty on high. For well nigh two thousand years *there*, He has remained. And there He *will* abide till the time of his coming and his kingdom arrives. He has never been overcome by His enemies. The gates of hell have never prevailed against him. The contents of the Jewish ark varied from time to time. There were things in it at one time which at another time had disappeared. Either the hand of violence had robbed it, or the hand of carelessness had neglected it. But it is not so with our ark. This is " the same yesterday, to-day, and forever." Nothing once embraced in it can ever be separated from it. All its precious, treasured contents are secure, beyond the utmost reach of fraud or violence. The Jewish ark of the covenant has passed away. It *was*,—but is not. But our ark is abiding still. It will abide forever. The covenant which it represents is everlasting. Its light, its joy, its grace and glory, yea, all its blessings and relationships are everlasting too. What a glorious shadow the Jewish ark of the covenant was! What a still more glorious substance the Christian ark of the covenant is! Believers in Jesus! children of this covenant! how well may you rejoice in your portion! What reason you have for abounding gladness! David esteemed the covenant of God's grace as " all his salvation and all his desire." But what did this covenant secure to David which it will not secure, as fully and effectually, to you? Has the circle of its benefits been in any wise restricted? No, there has been no restriction here; but there has been enlargement. The streams of covenant mercies run broader, and deeper, and fuller now than then. Oh, walk in the light of this covenant. Make full proof of its glorious privileges, and let your life bear witness to its sufficiency; its exhaustless power to satisfy and bless.

And my dear hearers who are not Christians, why will you remain unconnected with this glorious covenant? It contains only blessings to those who lay hold upon it. Yes, the richest and the choicest blessings to be found in the universe are garnered here. There are no real, substantial, abiding blessings outside of this covenant. To stand unconnected with this covenant is to stand unblest!

But you need not stand thus unconnected with it. God's gracious invitation, even to you, is—" Incline your ear, and come unto me; hear, and your soul shall live; and I will make an everlasting covenant with you; even the sure mercies of David." Is. lv. 3. If you remain unconnected with this covenant you will have only yourself to blame. May God graciously incline you to hear His voice, and come unto him that this blessed covenant may be "all your salvation, and all your desire forever! Amen!

CHAPTER VIII.

The Cherubim.

"And thou shalt make a mercy-seat of pure gold: two cubits and a half shall be the length thereof, and a cubit and a half the breadth thereof. And thou shalt make two cherubims of gold, of beaten work shalt thou make them, in the two ends of the mercy-seat. And make one cherub on the one end, and the other cherub on the other end; even of the mercy-seat shall ye make the cherubims on the two ends thereof. And the cherubims shall stretch forth their wings on high, covering the mercy-seat with their wings, and their faces shall look one to another; toward the mercy-seat shall the faces of the cherubims be. And thou shalt put the mercy-seat above upon the ark; and in the ark thou shalt put the testimony that I shall give thee. And there I will meet with thee, and I will commune with thee from above the mercy-seat, from between the two cherubims which are upon the ark of the testimony, of all things which I will give thee in commandment unto the children of Israel.—EXODUS, xxv. 17—22.

THE SHEKINAH AND CHERUBIM ABOVE THE MERCY-SEAT.
Jewish Tabernacle.

VII.

In our previous examination of this subject we have considered the nature and design of the tabernacle; and then, in detail, the different articles of furniture connected with it. Our last discourse was on the Ark, the great central object of interest connected with this heaven-devised structure. In that discourse we considered the ark of the covenant with reference to four things connected with it, viz.: *The veil which hung before it; The place in which it stood; The structure of the Ark, and its contents.* There remain two other points connected with it to be considered, viz.: *The Cherubim above the Ark; and the Mercy-seat with its glory.*

The first of these will constitute the theme of our present meditation. Let us now consider *the cherubim above the ark*. These are thus spoken of in our text: "And thou shalt make a mercy-seat of pure gold; and thou shalt make two cherubims of gold, of beaten work shalt thou make them, in the two ends of the mercy-seat. And make one cherub on the one end, and the other cherub on the other end; even of the mercy-seat shall ye make the cherubims in the two ends thereof. And the cherubims shall stretch forth their wings on high, covering the mercy-seat with their wings, and their faces shall look one to another; toward the mercy-seat shall the faces of the cherubims be. And thou shalt put the mercy-seat above upon the ark; and in the ark thou shalt put the testimony that I shall give thee. And there will I meet with thee, and will commune with thee from above the mercy-seat, from between the two cherubims which are upon the ark, of all things which I will give thee in commandment unto the children of Israel." Now you will observe that there is no description here given as to the form, or appearance of these cherubim, beyond the mention of their faces and of their wings. We are not informed who were represented, or what was intended by the cherubim. The widest possible diversity of opinion has existed among bible critics and commentators in regard to the meaning of these cherubim. It is not worth while to enter into any examination, or enumeration of these multifarious opinions. The most prevalent idea has been that the cherubim represented the angels. Their position on the ends of the ark, with their faces towards each other, and their earnest gaze, rivetted upon the mercy-seat, has been supposed to afford an illustration of the meaning of the apostle's words, when speaking of the interest manifested by the angels as students of the mysteries of redemption, he says—" which things the angels desire to look into."

But that it cannot be the angels, who are intended by these mysterious representations, is rendered perfectly clear when you consider that they were part and parcel of the ark itself. They were not something placed upon it, or added to it, but they were something made *of* it, or for it. They were beaten out of the very materials of the ark itself. The same gold which covered the mercy-seat was wrought out into the form of the cherubim. This could have no significancy as applied to the angels. They are indeed "ministering spirits unto the heirs of salvation," but they stand in no such intimate relation to the covenant of redemption as is indicated by the position which

THE CHERUBIM. 321

the cherubim occupied. There can be no question on this point. It is not the angels who are represented by the cherubim.

To whom then, or to what do they refer? *They are doubtless to be regarded, not perhaps as actual existences at all, but as symbols of the glorious qualities or attributes of Christ our Saviour, in carrying on the great work of our redemption, and of attributes or qualities which his ransomed people shall share with him in the glory of his heavenly kingdom.*

Now let us see what foundation the scriptures give us on which to base the position here assumed. We take it for granted that wherever we find the cherubim spoken of, or referred to, in scripture, they are to be regarded as always denoting the same order of beings or qualities. We are authorized then to bring to a focus, on the cherubim of the ark, whatever light we can gather from other parts of scripture respecting these same symbolical representations.

The most elaborate description of the cherubim, to be found anywhere in scripture, is that contained in the first chapter of Ezekiel, 5—14. Here we read—"Also, out of the midst thereof came the likeness of four living creatures." (That it is actually the cherubim the prophet is here describing is clear from chap. x. 20, where, after having had another vision of them, he winds up by saying—"This is the living creature that I saw by the river Chebar; and I knew that they were the cherubims.) Then the prophet proceeds thus in his description—"And this was their appearance, they had the likeness of a man. And every one had four faces, and every one had four wings. And their feet were straight feet; and the sole of their feet was like the sole of a calf's foot; and they sparkled like the color of burnished brass. And they had the hands of a man under their wings, on their four sides; and they four had their faces and their wings. Their wings were joined one to another. As for the likeness of their faces, they four had the face of a man, and the face of a lion on the right side; and they four had the face of an ox on the left side; and they four also had the face of an eagle. Thus were their faces; and their wings were stretched upward; two wings of every one were joined one to another, and two covered their bodies. As for the likeness of the living creatures, their appearance was like burning coals of fire, and like the appearance of lamps; and the fire was bright, and out of the fire went forth lightning. And the living creatures ran and returned like the appearance of a flash of lightning."

This is Ezekiel's description of the cherubim. You can hardly read it without having the conviction fastened upon your mind that it is a symbol, or representation of qualities, or attributes which the prophet is delineating rather than of organized beings, or actual existences. (A glance at the engraving, in which an attempt has been made to embody and represent to the eye, the description here given can hardly fail to deepen this conviction.)

But let us pass now from the visions of the river Chebar to those of the Isle of Patmos. Here our eye rests at once upon the following scene, depicted on the prophetic canvas: Rev. iv. 6—8. "And before the throne there was a sea of glass like unto crystal; and in the midst of the throne, and round about the throne, *were four beasts*, full of eyes behind and before." One can never read this description without a feeling of regret that our translators should have

THE CHERUBIM.

used the word "*beast,*" here. The Greek word in the original is the same as that in the Septuagint version of Ezekiel; and the sense would have been more properly given, if, here, as in the former place, it had been rendered by the phrase "*living creature.*" In quoting this passage further I shall give it this rendering: "And the first living creature was like a lion, and the second living creature was like a calf, the third had a face as a man, and the fourth was like a flying eagle. And the four living creatures had each of them six wings about him; and they were full of eyes within; and they rest not day and night, saying holy, holy, holy Lord God Almighty, which was, and is, and is to come." Here again we have the cherubim described. These are nearer the throne of Jehovah, with its incumbent majesty, than those seen by Ezekiel beside the river Chebar, and they are represented as having *six* wings instead of *four*, to denote the propriety of having their persons more fully veiled from the glance of that holy eye to which even the heavens are unclean. And what is the employment of these symbolic creatures, in the lofty position which they occupy? The apostle answers our inquiry satisfactorily. Rev. v. 8 10. "And when He had taken the book, the four living creatures, and four and twenty elders fell down before the Lamb, having, every one of them, harps and golden vials full of odors, which are the prayers of saints. And they sung a new song, saying, Thou art worthy to take the book, and to open the seals thereof; for Thou wast slain, and hast redeemed us to God by thy blood out of every kindred, and tongue, and people, and nation; and hast made us unto our God kings and priests; and we shall reign on the earth." Here we have the cherubim again. And the position which they are thus represented as occupying throws a flood of light on the part of the subject we are now considering. It goes very far to help us in the attempt to answer the question, in what sense are we to regard the cherubim? It shows us that the *Cherubim of the Tabernacle and Temple, and the living creatures of Ezekiel and St. John are all one and the same symbol.* This symbol does not represent the angels. But it does represent the qualities, or attributes of Christ our Saviour, exercised by Him in carrying on the great work of our redemption, and which his people will share with Him in the glory of His heavenly kingdom.

Now let us glance at the chief of these qualities as indicated by the appearance of the cherubim. As already stated, Moses gives no particular, or detailed description of the cherubim connected with the ark.

We are authorized, however, to associate with them the leading features found in Ezekiel's description. These are represented as bearing a quadriform figure, each having respectively the face of a lion, the face of an ox, the face of an eagle, and the face of a man. It is interesting, too, to remark in this connection that the fourfold countenance of the living creatures in Ezekiel's vision formed the standard of the tribes in their encampment in the wilderness. On each side of the sanctuary, or tabernacle were situated three of the twelve tribes. The standards of these several camps bore the same representations. There was the face of a lion on the right side; the face of an ox on the left; the face of an eagle in the front; and the face of a man in the rear. And what are the features of character indicated by these several faces which the cherubim bore? There is no difficulty in determining this. And it is a matter of great interest to us, as bearing at once upon our comfort for the present, and our hope for the future. These cherubims, as wrought out of the gold which covered the ark, stand before us as representatives of Christ, in the leading qualities which mark His character, as He carries on the work of our redemption. And whatever adds depth or clearness to our views of Christ's character has to do directly with our present comfort. Again these cherubims as connected with the ark of the covenant,—as associated intimately with Christ—and as placed upon the mercy-seat, where He pledges communion and fellowship with His people, are representatives of redeemed humanity, in the exalted position of blessedness and glory to which it will eventually be raised in the coming kingdom of the Son of Man. And whatever bears on this subject has to do, most intimately, with our hope for the future.

Let us look then at the qualities indicated by the fourfold faces of the Cherubim.

The first is the face of a man. This stands before us as the natural, and admitted index of *knowledge*, or *intelligence*. And this we know is a quality or attribute which Christ, in his position as our Redeemer, the crowning glory of our ark of the covenant, possesses in the fullest measure. "In Him are hid all the treasures of wisdom and knowledge." This is a broad, general declaration that covers the whole subject. But then what interesting statements we have scattered throughout the scriptures, giving us illustrations in detail of this truth! We have such illustrations when we read passages like these: "The Lord knoweth them that are his." "The Lord knoweth the way of the righteous." It was just this view of his Saviour's character on which David was meditating when he said—" Thou knowest my down-sitting, and mine uprising, Thou understandeth my thoughts afar off. Thou compassest my path, and my lying down, and art acquainted with *all my ways*." Again we read—" He knoweth our frame, He remembereth that we are but dust." The Lord knoweth how to deliver the godly out of temptation." In the language of the hymn—

" He knows what fierce temptations are,
   For He has felt the same."

In all these, and similar passages we have sweet and comforting illustrations of the knowledge and intelligence of Christ as an attribute of his character in working out our redemption. Believer in Jesus, when you read about " the face of a man " upon the cherubim, think of it as referring to Christ, and telling you, in expressive symbol, of the intimate acquaintance he has with you, the thorough knowledge he possesses of all your wants and weaknesses, and of everything that may be required to meet them.

But the Cherubim are representative of our humanity in its glorified state. And looking at it from this point of view we may gaze upon the " face of a man" in this mysterious symbol till it seems to have a voice and utterance, and to speak to us in eloquent terms of the grand disclosures, the marvellous unfoldings, of what are now hidden things, awaiting us in that bright world to which we are hastening. Just glance at some of the passages of God's word which may be regarded as bearing on this point,—pictorial illustrations of this aspect of the symbol before us. "In thy light we shall see light." Christian, this passage sets you down before the splendor of the everlasting throne. The radiance there prevailing has chased every cloud from your sky, every shadow from your path. Can you begin to imagine what the scope and fulness of your knowledge will be when this sweet promise is realized, and in God's light you see light? But I must quote without remark, or each separate point of our subject will be expanding into a sermon. "The light of the moon shall be as the light of the sun, and the light of the sun shall be seven-fold, as the light of seven days, in the day when the Lord bindeth up the breach of the people, and healeth the stroke of their wound." This, in the glowing imagery of Isaiah's gorgeous style, is a promise of the enlargement of knowledge awaiting God's people in the glory of their resurrection state. But we have the same truth presented in the solidity of plain, prose statements, as well as in the pomp of high-wrought poetry. The statement of our Saviour bears upon this point when He said to Peter—"What I do thou knowest not now, but thou shalt know hereafter." And so does his declaration to the apostles, when he affirmed so broadly— "There is nothing hid that shall not be manifest." But nothing can be more conclusive on this point than the full and absolute assertion of the apostle when he says to the Corinthians—"For now we see through a glass darkly; but then face to face; now we know in part, *but then shall we know, even as also we are known.*" 1 Cor. xiii. 12. Thus the "face of the man" upon the cherubim represents to us, in symbol, the knowledge that shall be possessed by the redeemed of Christ, in the glory of their heavenly state.

The second face which the cherubim bore was "the face of a lion." Two qualities are here indicated, viz., *courage* and *majesty*. The lion has ever been regarded, among all nations, as the natural representative of courage. *Bold as a lion,* is a simile admitted to be just, all over the world. And it was on this ground that England's heroic, and chivalrous king gained for himself the title, which he will wear to the end of time, of "Richard of the lion heart." Courage, true courage is an attribute or quality that has always commanded the respect and admiration of the world. It belongs by inheritance to the Anglo-Saxon race. It comes down to us from a noble ancestry in our father land. England's history, like our own, is full of noble instances illustrative of this fine quality. It was the display of this quality, connected with them, which gave such renown to Marathon, and Thermopylæ in ancient days,—to Crecy and Agincourt— Blenheim, Bunker Hill, and Waterloo, of later times; and which will weave into the same chaplet with them many names, rendered famous by the sad, sad conflict still in progress in our own land. But the great Captain of our salvation, in the campaign which He undertook, when he resolved to put down the rebellion which had broken out in this province of His Father's dominions, afforded the grandest exhibition of this noble quality, which, the world, or the universe has ever witnessed. This campaign is not yet finished. The history of it has not yet been written. When this conflict is over; when this rebellion is put down, and the history of it is written out, it may be by the combined agency of some of those "holy men of old," who once "spoke and wrote as they were moved by the Holy Ghost—by David, and Isaiah, and Ezekiel, or by Peter, and John, and Paul, there will be one scene, around which will be spread a halo of moral grandeur, reflected from the peerless heroism of the Captain of our salvation, which will throw into the shade all other examples of courage recorded in the annals of the world, or of the universe. Gethsemane was the theatre of that transaction. The stake at issue was the souls of a race of ruined creatures. The combatants were, on the one side, the embattled powers of darkness, led on by Satan, an arch-angel fallen; on the other side stood—Jesus, alone. "Of the people there were none with Him." "He came to his own, but his own received him not." In that hour of his greatest need " all his disciples forsook him and fled." The angel hosts were kept aloof, though they would gladly have been at his side amidst the conflict. Even his Father withdrew his face and forsook him then. He stood in the Thermopylæ of the universe,—*alone*. He knew that hell had emptied itself to meet Him there. He knew the number, the power, the fierceness of his foes. Yet, unappalled, he marched steadily onward to the struggle. He met the foe single-handed. With undaunted spirit he bore the tremendous shock; and though He fell in the conflict, yet *He conquered as He fell.* " He spoiled principalities and powers," and " opened the kingdom of heaven to all believers." Here was courage without a parallel. Here we see " the Lion of the tribe of Judah" acting out his true character. And this courage of our great chief is indicated by " the face of a lion," as seen upon the cherubim.

And this quality is a characteristic of redeemed humanity as well as of Him who redeemed it. It applies to true Christians even now. " The righteous are bold as a lion," says the wise man. But it will apply to them much more truly hereafter. It is said of them that—" they shall have boldness in the day of judgment." This is the

THE CHERUBIM.

very highest exercise of this most noble quality. In this relation it is not a natural, but a gracious attribute of character. It results from connection with Christ, and the covenant of his salvation. It is beautifully explained by the language of the hymn which represents the believer as saying—

> "Jesus, thy blood and righteousness
> My beauty are, my glorious dress—
> Midst flaming worlds in these array'd
> With joy will I lift up my head."

But "the face of the lion" was indicative of *majesty* as well as courage. Majesty is not an assumed thing. It is not a necessary attendant of official position; but it is the natural result of the possession of pre-eminent excellences. There is the halo round the sun for instance; this is nothing else than the glory created by the shining of its own rays. And it is just so with the majesty of Christ. This is the halo round his character—the radiance formed by the shining forth of His own glory. He is "the brightness of the Father's glory, and the express image of His person." He is "the chief among ten thousand, and altogether lovely." He is the substance of which all the glories of the material creation are but shadows. Matchless courage and peerless majesty are his. And this is indicated by the face of the lion upon the cherubim.

But this is a quality, too, which will mark the condition of the redeemed, in the glory of their future state. True, with them it will not be an inherited, but an imparted quality. In themselves, of their own, they have nothing attractive, or majestic. But they do have that imparted to them, by their glorious Lord, which makes them so. Hence, speaking to His Church, Jesus says: "Thy *beauty* was *perfect* through my comeliness, which I put upon thee." None will deny that *perfect beauty* is a majestic thing. This attribute of the character of the redeemed in their future state is fully sustained by passages like these: "Then shall the righteous shine forth as the sun in the kingdom of their Father." "Thou shalt be a crown of glory in the hand of the Lord, and a royal diadem in the hand of thy God." Solomon represented the Church of the Redeemed, "looking forth as the morning, beautiful as Tirzah, comely as Jerusalem, fair as the sun, clear as the moon, and terrible as an army with banners." All these expressions prove that majesty, of the noblest order, will be a feature of character marking the condition of the redeemed in glory. Courage and majesty will pertain to them, as to their glorious Lord, and "the face of the lion" upon the cherubim is the symbol of these qualities.

The third face which the cherubim bore

was "*the face of an ox.*" The quality which this represents is, manifestly, that of *strength for service.* " That our oxen may be *strong to labor,*" says the Psalmist, when praying for temporal blessings on the people. And Solomon says: "Much increase is by the *strength* of the ox." And strength, we know, is a glorious attribute of our divine Redeemer. It is one which he possesses, too, in absolute perfection. In speaking of Him, in connection with the work to which He had appointed him, God, the Father, says: "I have laid help upon one who is mighty." It is of Him the prophet is speaking when he says to Israel,—" Trust ye in the Lord forever; for in the Lord Jehovah is everlasting strength." He is " the Creator of the ends of the earth, who fainteth not, neither is weary." He has " power over all flesh to give eternal life to as many as the Father hath given him." " He is able to save unto the uttermost them that come unto God by him." "All power in heaven and on earth is given unto him." "Nothing is impossible with him." "He is mighty to save, and strong to deliver." "The government" of the Church and of the universe "is upon His shoulder." It is an easy yoke, a light burden for Him to bear, because He is girded with omnipotence. He has exhaustless strength for the service he has undertaken. "The face of the ox," as represented on the mysterious cherubim, was a significant symbol of this attribute of our Saviour's character.

But it symbolized the same quality as marking the condition of his people in that glorious kingdom to which it is His gracious purpose eventually to bring them. It is the covenant privilege of the redeemed, even now, in the imperfection of this fallen state, to be "strong in the Lord, and in the power of his might." They "take hold of his strength," and this enables them to mount up with wings as eagles, to " run and not be weary, to walk and not faint." But the ark, and the cherubim upon it, point us onward to the heavenly world. It is a quality, or property, of redeemed humanity in the glory of the resurrection state to which the symbol now before us refers.

That will be an active state,—a condition of the most exalted and glorious service. It is when St. John is in the midst of his most transporting description of the grandeur and blessedness of that state,—when the vision of the heavenly Jerusalem is clearly unfolded to his view, and he is gazing enraptured on that city of the skies, as it sparkles in its ineffable beauty before him,—that he says of those who shall be favored to enter there—" *His servants shall serve Him.*" Directly after he adds—" and there shall be no night there." The service of that blessed state will be an unceasing service. When he is describing the living creatures, the cherubim, in another of the Apocalyptic visions, he says of them, that " they rest not day and night, saying, Holy, Holy, Holy is the Lord God Almighty." And yet we are told elsewhere of the redeemed in glory that they " enter into rest.' There is no discrepancy between these statements. It is true of the redeemed that they will serve God day and night, *i. e.*, unceasingly, for " there is no night there." And it is true, at the same time, that they will " enter into rest." Ceaseless activity is not compatible with a state of rest *here*, but it will be *there*. There will be bliss in every service, and rest in every motion. And this gives us the most striking view we can have of the strength, the amazing might, the tireless vigor which will be girding every faculty of the ransomed in the kingdom of their Father. In the striking language of the prophet, "They will be strong and do exploits." And this idea is embodied in "the face of the ox" described upon the cherubim.

The last face associated with this mysterious symbol was "the face of an eagle."

Now, one of the things for which an eagle is remarkable, is its *keenness of vision*. God says of the eagle—"From the crag of the rock she seeketh her prey; and her eyes behold *afar off*." Our Saviour said—"Wheresoever the carcass is there will the eagles be gathered together." In confirmation of this, Oriental travellers tell us that, in the progress of their caravans, when a horse or a camel dies, it scarcely falls to the ground before the eagles sight their prey and light upon it. And all the power, or quickness of vision, which the eagle possesses is but a symbol of a corresponding attribute of character pertaining to Christ. His eyes are in every place. " He seeth the end from the beginning." " He knoweth our necessities before we ask." When Satan desired to have Peter "that he might sift him as wheat," and laid his snare for him accordingly, Jesus saw it all, and gave timely warning of it to his impulsive, and honest-hearted, but self-confident disciple. He saw the approach of the Roman armies to Jerusalem fifty years before they came, and He left wise counsel for his people, to guide their steps in that emergency, and guard them from that danger. " Wonderful Counsellor" was part of the name the prophet gave Him before his birth, and it is His name still. His quick, unslumbering eye surveys every path along which His people tread. He sees the dangers that beset them, the snares in secret laid for their harm, and

He guards them from those dangers, and delivers them from those snares. "The face of the eagle," on the cherubim, gives us, in symbol, the assurance of this quality in our glorious Lord. It is a comforting assurance.

But how does this apply to the redeemed in the glory of their future state? This is not a point on which any definite, or explicit information is given us in the Scriptures. But there are two passages which, when brought together, and looked at, in the light of this subject, are, to say the least, very suggestive. We find St. Paul speaking to the Hebrew Christians, of "the powers of the world to come." Heb., vi. 5. We cannot stop now to discuss this passage critically. But there can be no question that it refers to faculties, attributes, or qualities, mental, moral, or physical, to be possessed by the redeemed of Christ amidst the glory and blessedness of the world to come. And this being assumed we are prepared for the other passage in question. This is found in Isaiah xxxiii. 17. Here, the prophet, after speaking of the present privileges of the child of the covenant, is led on to glance at his position in the future. He says: " Thine eyes shall see the king in his beauty; they shall behold the land that is very far off." Now I venture not to dogmatize about this passage. I would not affirm positively that it is intended to teach this, or that, or the other idea respecting the condition of the redeemed in glory; but when I bear in mind how marvellously exalted that position will be; when I remember St. Paul's intimation about "the powers of the world to come," and then come back and look upon Ezekiel's sketch of the cherubim with its eagle eye—Oh, I feel that, if I am a believer in Jesus, I have here a promise, in symbol, of such an enlargement of perceptive faculty and power of vision as quite passes my capacity at present to comprehend.

But *quickness of motion*, or *speed of flight* is another characteristic quality of the eagle.

In one of the terrific denunciations which Moses left on record, for Israel's admonition, he says, "The Lord shall bring a nation upon thee from the ends of the earth, *as swift as the eagle flieth.*" Nothing can be more expressive of celerity or despatch in action than is this language. And this we know is a quality which strikingly marks the character of Christ in carrying on the work of our redemption. It was so when He was on earth. What He did for those who sought His gracious intervention, He did quickly. How often, when the blind appealed to Him, we read that "*immediately* their eyes were opened!" How often when the poor, forlorn lepers invoked his healing power, we read that "*immediately their leprosy was cleansed.*" This quality marks His character still. It is only by the practical development of it that He can make good His word when He engages in one place to be to all His people "a very present help in trouble;" and in another to be always "a God at hand, and not afar off;" or when, in still another place, His promise runs—"Before they call I will answer, and while they are yet speaking I will hear." It is clearly manifest how "the face of the eagle" upon the cherubim points to this feature of our Lord's character.

But what bearing has this on the position of the redeemed in glory? I answer, a very natural and necessary bearing. It teaches us that quickness of motion, or speed of flight, will be a characteristic of that state. This idea is more distinctly taught us, than any other of which we have spoken, in the passage from Ezekiel to which we have referred. For, observe that in the fourteenth verse the prophet tells us, that " the living creatures ran and returned as the appearance of a flash of lightning." The capacity to move with lightning speed, with the quickness of thought, this, we are here taught, will be one of the features marking the condition of the redeemed in glory—one of " the powers of the world to come." Their position as kings and priests unto God and the Lamb will require this. In that position they will be officiating, as channels of communication, between their triumphant Redeemer, in that New Jerusalem of which He will be the light and glory, and the saved nations who shall then be peopling the earth. To those nations the resurrection saints will stand in a relation analogous to that which the angels now sustain towards the heirs of salvation when they act to them as

THE CHERUBIM. 353

ministering spirits; and in a position like this the power, or faculty, of which we now speak, will be an absolute necessity. But we are assured of their possession of this power, when we gaze upon the face of the eagle which the cherubim bore.

Thus we have attempted to point out the significance of this symbol in its bearing, both on the qualities which characterize our blessed Lord in the work He is now carrying on, and which will mark the condition of His people in the glory and blessedness of his promised kingdom.

In conclusion—*How glorious are the prospects for the future which the Gospel unfolds to believers in Jesus!* We only speak now of these prospects as they appear in the light of our present subject. The cherubim, with their four-fold faces, stand before us as significant symbols of the noble qualities which mark the character of our Saviour now, and which all His people will share with Him hereafter. "We know," says the apostle, "that when He shall appear *we shall be like Him*." How impressive such a statement becomes in the light which shines upon it from the mysterious cherubim! To be like Him in knowledge, as indicated by the face of a man; like him in courage and majesty, as indicated by the face of a lion; like him in strength for service, as indicated by the face of an ox; like him in power of vision and swiftness of motion, as indicated by the face of an eagle;—in a word, like him in every respect in which a creature *can be* like the Creator—what a destiny is this! Yet, Christian, this is the inheritance reserved for you! When Jesus was speaking of His people in their resurrection state, He said they should be "*as the angels.*" Here we see how this statement will be realized. Glorified men will be equal to the angels in most respects; but in some respects they will be better off than even the angels themselves. The angels must stand forever on the ground of their own righteousness,—a creature's righteousness; but redeemed men will stand forever, and be exalted in the righteousness of Christ—a finished, perfect, and transcendently glorious righteousness. The angels can stand no more closely related to Christ than any other unfallen creatures; but redeemed men will be more intimately related to Him than any other creatures in the universe. For "He took not on Him the nature of angels," but,—glorious thought;—"He took on him the seed of Abraham." Jehovah Jesus wears our nature on the throne of the universe. The mantle of humanity is on Him there. How near this brings us to Him! And then there is one other point in which our position will be superior to theirs. The angels will sing the anthem of creation, and of preservation,—but the anthem of redemption, they will not be able to sing. "Worthy the Lamb, for He was slain *for us*,"—will not be true of them. This is a note in the music of the upper sanctuary too high for angel harps to strike. The ransomed of earth alone will be able to reach this lofty strain. Believers in Jesus, this is your portion! What love you owe! what praise; what gratitude! what devotion! to Him, who, by His suffering and death, has opened the pathway for you to this glorious inheritance! Oh, then—

> "Since *words* can never measure,
> Let your *life* show forth His praise!"

And what a motive this subject suggests, to urge you to seek an interest in Jesus, my dear hearers who are yet strangers to Him. Our ruined nature can find perfection and enduring blessedness only in Christ. The path of life starts from His cross. All that is pure and noble, all that is elevated and enduring, in the development of humanity is to be found in Jesus. The blessing, the glory, the immortality for which our spirits pine can only be secured in Him. Seek Jesus and be pardoned. Seek Jesus and be transformed. Seek Jesus and be happy. Seek Jesus and be saved.

> "In Him you'll then abide,
>   And sweet shall be your rest,
> With every longing satisfied,
>   In full salvation blest."

CHAPTER IX.

The Mercy-seat.

"And thou shalt make a mercy-seat of pure gold: two cubits and a half shall be the length thereof, and a cubit and a half the breadth thereof. And thou shalt put the mercy-seat above upon the ark; and in the ark thou shalt put the testimony that I shall give thee. And there will I meet with thee, and I will commune with thee from above the mercy-seat, from between the two cherubims which are upon the ark of the testimony, of all things which I will give thee in commandment unto the children of Israel.—EXODUS, xxv. 17, 21, 22.

IX.

WHEN Moses made the tabernacle he began where we leave off, in our consideration of it. The ark of the covenant, the last article of the sacred furniture to claim our attention, is the first thing described by him, in his account of the tabernacle, and it was doubtless that which first engaged his thoughts, in the erection of the heaven-appointed structure. He finished this, in all its mysterious beauty, before proceeding further. He then took up, in the order of their relation to the ark, the other articles pertaining to the tabernacle. It was natural for Moses to pursue the course he did; and equally natural for us to have pursued the opposite course. In the erection of a building it is natural to begin with the foundation; but in *describing* the same building it would be very unnatural to begin at the same point. We have imagined ourselves to be strangers, on a visit of inquiry and observation to the camp of Israel, and the august and impressive arrangement for divine worship connected with its tabernacle. We have attempted to describe the tabernacle and its furniture as it would have appeared to a person thus approaching it. We have taken up, and considered the different objects connected with it, in the order in which they would have presented themselves, under such circumstances.

From the outer door of the court of the tabernacle, we have advanced, step by step, till at last, with solemn awe, we have reached the Most Holy Place, where the ark, with its overshadowing cherubim, has stood before us for consideration.

We have taken up five several points of inquiry in connection with the ark. We have noticed in succession—the veil which hung before the ark; the place in which the ark stood; its structure; its contents; the cherubim above it; and now, one other point alone remains to be considered, viz.: *The Mercy-seat and its glory.*

This is the subject of our present meditation. *In dwelling on this subject we may consider what the mercy-seat was literally—and what it was typically, or symbolically.*

In its simple, literal acceptation, the mercy-seat denoted merely the cover, or lid of the ark. In the words which God addressed to Moses, respecting it, in our text, it is thus described: "And thou shalt make a mercy-seat of pure gold: two cubits and a half shall be the length thereof, and a cubit and a half the breadth thereof. And thou shalt put the Mercy-seat above, upon the ark."

There is very little to say under this first branch of our subject. Taken in its primary or literal sense the mercy-seat was nothing else than the lid or covering of the ark. It was made of pure gold. The rest of the ark was made of shittim-wood, overlaid with gold. But there was no wood about the mercy-seat. It was all of gold, and only of gold. We are not told why such a difference was ordained to exist between this portion of the ark and the remainder of it. It does not become us curiously to pry into matters that God has not seen fit to reveal, nor aim to be wise above what is written. But if, as we have before supposed, the wood and the gold represented the two natures of our Saviour, then, when the mercy-seat is described, there would seem to be a peculiar significancy in representing it as composed of gold alone, for the relations there to be sustained by God to His people, as we shall see presently, were such as pertained peculiarly to the Godhead, and not to the humanity.

It is worthy of notice that the word in the Hebrew rendered mercy-seat here, comes from the old root *caphar,* or *cophar,* which signifies to hide, or cover, and is doubtless the origin of our English word *cover.* Literally the mercy-seat was the covering of the ark.

But our chief concern is with the mercy-seat, *in its typical or symbolical meaning.* And there is perhaps no better or more satisfactory way of getting at this meaning than by looking for a moment at the true sense of the word in the Hebrew and Greek Scriptures, rendered respectively in our English version by the term mercy-seat. In the Hebrew Bible, it is the word *caphareth,* or *cophareth,* from the word *copher.* This, in its strict or primary sense, means *to atone* for sin, *to expiate,* or *forgive* sin. In its secondary, or metaphorical sense, it means *to cover* sin. And this gives us the true scriptural sense of pardon as resulting from an atonement. It is the putting away, or hiding of sin—the causing of it not to appear. Hence, says the Psalmist—" Blessed is he whose transgression is forgiven; whose sin is *covered.* The word used in the Septuagint, and in the Greek version of the New Testament, to translate the term, which in Hebrew means simply a cover, is ἱλαστήριον —*ilastarion,* which means an " expiatory," or a " propitiatory," denoting that by which atonement is made, or pardon obtained, or in other words, by which sin is covered. And this you will see had a peculiar significancy as applied to the mercy-seat, when

THE MERCY-SEAT. 367

you bear in mind the solemn service performed every year in connection with it. On the great day of atonement the high-priest entered the Most Holy Place with the blood of a slaughtered victim. This blood was sprinkled on the mercy-seat. By doing this he "made an atonement for the sins of the people." And in this way that golden lid of the ark, became the "propitiatory,"— *i. e.*, the atoning cover of the sins of the people. You will see from this that though the term *mercy-seat* is a sweet and beautiful term, and one that we cannot but love, still it does not give us a good translation of the idea involved in the metaphorical sense of the original Hebrew, and still less of the Greek word *ilastarion*. It rather carries off our minds from the idea conveyed by the words used in the original scriptures. The cover of the ark was doubtless the *seat of mercy;* but then it was mercy conferred through an act of expiation, through the blood of an atoning sacrifice. Our word *mercy-seat* intimates nothing of this kind. The word in the Hebrew Bible for which this term is put, told distinctly of bloodshed, or expiation made. And the Greek word did the same, but our word carries with it nothing to suggest this idea. At each end of this mercy-seat, or cover of the ark, was a cherub of beaten gold. These stretched out their wings towards each other, and formed a kind of throne, where the Lord was considered as sitting. Hence the Psalmist in addressing him exclaims—" Oh, Shepherd of Israel, Thou that dwellest between the cherubims, shine forth." And it is when contemplated from this point of view especially, that the mercy-seat, or cover of the Jewish ark, points us directly to Christ. " *He* is the propitiation for our sins, and not for *ours* only, but also for the sins of the whole world." Our atonement is in Him. He is at once our mercy-seat, and our reconciled God, " dwelling between the cherubims," and ready to shine forth in pardoning love, and saving grace and mercy to poor sinners. If we had a word denoting—*reconciliation-seat*, or *residence*, we should come nearer to the idea of the original scriptures on this subject. What we call the mercy-seat was the station of a person understood to be constantly present there, that he might be reconciled to those who entreated him. Thus the space above the lid, or cover of the ark, and between the cherubim, was the reconciliation-seat, the place of atonement for the Jewish people, where God engaged to meet them, to be at peace with them, and impart to them his mercy. But now the apostle declares—Rom. iii. 25—that "God hath set forth Jesus Christ to be a propitiation "—(the

Greek word here is *ilastarion*, the same that is used in the Septuagint version of the Old Testament for the mercy-seat)—*i. e.*, to be a reconciliation-seat, or residence "through faith in his blood." And thus we are taught that as God was understood to be constantly on the mercy-seat of old, as the place where reconciliation was to be sought, and mercy obtained; so now He is in Christ, who is His residence for the same blessed purpose. Thus we are told that "God is *in* Christ, reconciling the world unto Himself." Our mercy-seat, our reconciliation-residence is Jesus, the divine Saviour, the God-man mediator. And all the typical teachings of this branch of our subject may be drawn out in the attempt to answer one question, viz.— *what sort of a mercy-seat have we in Christ?*

In replying to this inquiry, I desire to show that we have in Christ, *in the first place, an authorized mercy-seat.*

THE MERCY-SEAT.

We have a mercy-seat based on law. This was significantly intimated in the Jewish ark, by the fact that the tables of the law were placed in the ark. The golden mercy-seat of the tabernacle might be said to have rested on the law. This was a very suggestive circumstance. And it is full of instruction in its symbolical bearings. It tells us that our mercy-seat is *based on law*. He who occupies this mercy-seat is " a *just* God and a Saviour." No violence is done to any principle of honor, or of justice in the government of the universe by the dispensing of grace from this mercy-seat. The divine law is magnified and made honorable. Every attribute of the divine character is vindicated. He who occupies this mercy-seat is one who "loveth righteousness, and hateth iniquity." "The sceptre of his kingdom is a right sceptre." God the Father has weighed his work in the balances of the heavenly sanctuary, and put the mark of His approbation upon it. Again and again, when Jesus was on earth, working out our redemption, the voice from the eternal throne was heard proclaiming: "This is my beloved Son, in whom I am well pleased." And when the work of Him who sits upon the mercy-seat shall be displayed, in the glory of its final consummation, before a beholding universe, the approving plaudit extorted from the adoring multitude will be —" Great and marvellous are thy works, Lord God Almighty! *Just* and true are thy ways, thou King of saints!" The mercy-seat to which we come in Christ is an authorized mercy-seat. Not only the goodness and love of God are gratified by it; but his wisdom, his truth, his holiness, and his justice even, yea, all the severer attributes of his character are honored by it, and give their delighted testimony in its support. It is an authorized mercy-seat to which we are invited.

But I observe secondly of the mercy-seat which we are bidden to approach in Christ, that it is an ENCOURAGING MERCY-SEAT.

This aspect of it comes out to view when we reflect how the lid of the ark covered the law as it was a broken law. The law of God, deposited in the Jewish ark, had a two-fold point of view from which it was to be contemplated, one of these had reference to Christ, the other had reference to his people. As it stood connected with Christ it was a law unbroken. He had delighted to do it. He had met its every requirement. He had kept and honored it, most perfectly, down even to the least jot, or tittle of its demands. And when contemplated from this point of view, the law was in the ark, as we have seen, to uphold and sustain the mercy-seat which was over it.

But the law in the ark stood connected with Christ's people, as well as with Himself. And when looked at from this point of view, it presents itself only in one aspect, and that is as *a broken law*. Looked at in our natural state, out of Christ, we can only know and think of God's law as a law which we have broken. In letter, or in spirit, we have broken every precept of it. We have done this not once or twice, or occasionally, but over and over again. Our natural lives have been *made up* of breaches of the law. Continued existence with us was a continued violation of it. We have failed entirely of obedience to it. We have come short of all its requirements. We have incurred all its penalties. It has but one voice in which to speak respecting us, and that is the voice of unsparing, terrible condemnation. The scattered fragments of this broken law stare us in the face, and lie right in the way of our return to God. There can be no peace, nor hope, nor comfort for us till this broken law is taken away. We can have no access to God, nor joy in the thought of Him till this is done. But how can this be done? Who can take this terrible law out of our way? Who can gather up its broken fragments and hide them, or cover them up so that God's all-searching eye shall no longer see them? Jesus can do this. He *has* done it for his people. See how beautifully this was symbolized in the ark as it stood within the Jewish tabernacle! There, in the ark, is the law which the people have broken. But see, over it is the lid of gold, sprinkled with the blood of the atoning sacrifice. That covers entirely the broken law. When God looks upon that mercy-seat his eye rests not upon the broken law, but only on the burnished gold with its sprinkled blood. And here we see, how beautifully! the shadow, of which we have the glorious substance in Christ. He came to "put away sin by the sacrifice of himself." And he did it. And now of his people it is said, that "their lives are hid with Christ in God." They are "accepted in the beloved;" they are "complete in Him." God does not impute unto them their trespasses. Their sins are "blotted out;" "put away;" "hid;" "covered." This is the point of view from which to contemplate, in its true meaning, those marvellous words in which it is declared of God's people that—"He hath not beheld iniquity in Jacob, neither hath He seen perverseness in Israel." There are no more wonderful words in the Bible than these. And the golden mercy-seat, shutting out from view the law which we have broken, gives us the clew to their meaning. You know when you look at any object through a piece of colored glass how naturally it assumes the hue of the medium through which you are looking at it. Now, Christ, in the glory of his finished righteousness, is the medium through which God looks at all His believing children. He sees them only "in the face of his anointed." Hence it is said of believers in Christ that "they are righteous" in God's sight, "even as He," *i. e.*, Christ "is righteous." I. John, iii. 7. And again we read that— "*as He is, so are we.*" I. John, iv. 17. Surely then, as teaching us a truth so precious as this, we may well say of the mercy-seat which we find in Christ that it is an *encouraging* mercy-seat.

But thirdly I observe respecting this mercy-seat that it is FULL OF PRIVILEGE FOR THE PRESENT.

To the Jew the golden mercy-seat above the ark was the place of the oracle, the appointed channel of communication between God and the people. God said to Him— "There will I meet with thee, and I will commune with thee from above the mercy-seat." As Israel journeyed through the wilderness, when any emergency arose involving the interests or welfare of the people, Moses, as their head, or representative, was accustomed to enter the tabernacle, and spread his case before the Lord, and receive instruction suited to his circumstances from Him "who dwelt between the cherubim."

But what Moses did on special occasions for the nation of Israel, the people of God may now do, each one for himself, on all occasions. Christ Jesus is our mercy-seat, and the way of access to Him is open at all times. It is through Him we have fellowship with the Father, and from Him that we receive all the help and grace we need.

THE MERCY-SEAT. 379

It is impossible to overstate the preciousness of the mercy-seat, or to estimate too highly the privilege of access to it. Suppose you were travelling in a foreign land. You are cut off from intercourse with all whom you most love on earth. There is only one channel through which you can hear from home, and obtain the supply of all that is necessary to meet your daily wants, how precious that channel of communication would be to you! How you would prize it! What store you would set by it! How anxious and careful you would be to keep it open! The thought of having it interrupted, or cut off, would be insupportable to you. Yet this is but a faint image of the Christian's position here in the world, and of the relation of the mercy-seat to him. "He is far off from his home." He is a pilgrim and stranger in a foreign land. His home, with all the objects of his supreme affection, is above. And it is only through Christ upon the mercy-seat that he can keep up communication with home, and obtain thence the supplies on which he depends. All that he needs for body and for soul, for time and for eternity, comes to him through Christ. He esteems it the very choicest of his privileges, the crowning blessing of his pilgrimage that he has access to the mercy-seat. To know that from all parts of the earth, wherever he may be,—at all times, and under all circumstances—the way to the mercy-seat lies open,—and that with all his burdens, griefs, anxieties, and cares he may come to it, and be sure of a hearing ear, a sympathizing heart, and a helping hand; this makes the thought of the mercy-seat unspeakably precious to him. He is ready to unite with believers everywhere, and say, as the language of true Christian experience—

THE MERCY-SEAT. 381

"This is the place where Jesus sheds
The oil of gladness on our heads,
The place of all on earth most sweet;
The precious, blood-bought mercy-seat.

Here, here, on eagle's wings we soar,
And sense and sin molest no more;
And heaven comes down our souls to greet,
While glory crowns the mercy-seat."

Full of privilege for the present is our mercy-seat.

There is only one other point of view from which we may glance at the mercy-seat, and thus contemplated it shines before us as BRIGHT WITH HOPE FOR THE FUTURE.

Over the Jewish mercy-seat there rested the mysterious shekinah—the cloud of the divine presence. That cloud served in part to reveal, but much more to hide the fulness of the divine glory. A few feeble rays of that glory shone forth there from time to time. But these were as nothing,—but a drop to the unmeasured depths of the ocean, compared with what remained unrevealed of the character and glory of God. But that cloud upon the mercy-seat pointed to Christ. He is the true shekinah. Hence it was said of Him when He appeared on earth—" we beheld His glory—the glory as of the only begotten of the Father—full of grace and truth." All that we know of the glory of the divine character we know through Christ. For "God who commanded the light to shine out of darkness, hath shined in our hearts to give the light of the knowledge of the glory of God in the face of Jesus Christ." We have reason to doubt if the least portion of that glory has ever been revealed through any other channel. What Jesus said when he was on earth remains a truth in the broadest and the fullest sense: "The only begotten Son, who was in the bosom of the Father, *He hath declared Him.*" But then He had only made a beginning in this work of declaring the Father. He said Himself—"I *have* declared thy name, and *will* declare it." The former part of this statement refers to the past and present agency of Christ in making God known to his people; the latter part of it refers to his agency in the future in carrying on this same glorious work. He told his disciples that the time was coming "when He would show them *plainly* of the Father." He says in the 22d Psalm—"I will declare thy name unto my brethren; in the midst of the Church will I sing praise unto thee." This represents our glorious Saviour in the midst of his chosen people, the church triumphant in heaven, illustrating and making plain to them the mysteries of the Godhead. And all this is significantly shadowed forth, when God points to the mercy-seat, with the shekinah above it, and says—" *there* will I meet with thee, and commune with thee." Thus contemplated, the cloud upon the Jewish mercy-seat becomes bright with hope for the future. As the eyes of the Jewish high-priest rested on that cloud they never witnessed anything more than a faint raying forth of the glory which was contained there. But "the face of Jesus Christ," who is the cloud upon our mercy-seat, is destined to become all-radiant with its manifestations of the ineffable glories of the God-head. Hitherto it has always been true of Jehovah, that—"verily He is a God that *hideth* Himself." But the time cometh, when of all that pertains to the character and work of God, it may be said—"there hath been nothing hid that will not be made manifest." "What we know not now we shall know hereafter." The true shekinah upon the mercy-seat will have no single dark point connected with it. Over all its outspread surface the cloud will be lighted up with the splendors of divinity. You have often seen a mass of clouds in the western sky, unillumined by the sun's rays, as the day was drawing to a close. You know how dark and unattractive that mass appeared. But presently you see the sun pass behind it, and what a wondrous transformation is wrought in its appearance! How radiant the whole mass becomes! How every point in it glows and sparkles with the splendors of the sun that shines through it! So will it be with the cloud upon our mercy-seat. When Jesus was on earth the coarse garments of humanity were upon Him. Then the shekinah cloud was dark. But the redeemed shall look upon that cloud again amidst the glory of the heavenly kingdom. Then all darkness will have passed away. The sun of uncreated deity will be pouring all its brightness through it. How transcendently glorious the cloud upon the mercy-seat will then appear! The scene of the transfiguration was intended as a faint foreshadowing of the glory that will finally be revealed in Christ. A further illustration of what will be disclosed by the cloud upon our mercy-seat we have in the sight which met the enraptured gaze of the Evangelist, when he had his vision of the heavenly world. He saw the New Jerusalem, the abode of the redeemed, shining in all the radiance of its loveliness; but there was neither sun nor moon to shed their rays upon it, for "the Lamb was the light thereof." Who may imagine what the rapture of the redeemed will be when they thus look upon that Saviour who is the object of their supreme affection? This will be to "see *Him as He is*." Then the Saviour's prayer will be answered: "Father, I will that they also whom Thou hast given me, be with me, where I am—*that they may be-*

hold my glory! That will be the highest point of happiness—the perfection of bliss.

> " Forever to behold Him shine,
> Forevermore to call Him mine,
>   And see Him still before me!
> Forever on His face to gaze,
> And meet His full assembled rays,
> While all the Father He displays
>   To all the saints in glory!"

This will be to " see the king in his beauty." And anticipating such a portion as his inheritance forever, well might the Psalmist say—" when I awake in thy likeness I shall be *satisfied* with it."

And thus contemplating Christ as our mercy-seat, we see how truly we *have in Him an authorized mercy-seat—an encouraging mercy-seat—a mercy-seat full of privilege for the present; and bright with hope for the future.*

And now we have brought our meditations on this most instructive subject to a close. I have never been engaged in a course of sermons that have been, to my own mind, more replete with profitable suggestions than these upon the tabernacle. And the chief source of interest and profit in them has been found in the direct and intimate relation of the great theme, which has furnished them, to Christ and his salvation. If there is one New Testament text which, more than any other, the tabernacle and its furniture may be regarded as illustrating, it is that in which the apostle declares that—*"Christ is all, and in all."*

"Such," says an English writer, "is the grand central truth in which the many trains of thought springing from the tabernacle-architecture converge and terminate. The sanctuaries, and the vessels of the sanctuaries all speak this one voice. The altar tells of Christ as the sacrifice for sin; the laver of Christ as the giver of the Spirit; the candlestick shines on the shew-bread and reveals Christ: the table lifts up Christ in the eyes of believers; the censer is full of Christ in his intercession, and the mercy-seat is Christ, the great Mediator. All speak of Christ, for Christ is all."

"Christ is the hope of the world. In Him, in Him alone, there is mercy for the rebellious. His streaming blood, his regenerating Spirit, make the grand distinction between earth and hell. The hope of the world is in the cross. When the world is blessed, it will be blessed in Christ. He is the hope of salvation for each individual sinner, and for a sinful world. No Christ, no hope."

"Christ is the joy of the church. Every blessing which believers enjoy flows from Christ. He is the support and strength of his people. He enlightens and warms them with his Spirit. He kindles in their breast the fire of devotion, and presents their prayers and praises before the throne. Christ is the believer's joy, his delight, his song."

"Christ is the glory of heaven. His presence makes it what it is. Without him, as the mercy-seat and the High-priest, heaven would be no heaven to us. He prepares it for us, no less than us for it. He shrouds the excessive brightness of the Godhead, satisfies the Father's insulted justice, encircles the throne with the rainbow of love, that pardoned and justified, sanctified and glorified sinners may enter the holiest without fear, mingling with cherubim and seraphim, with 'angels and arch-angels, and all the company of heaven.' Yes, the words from the New Testament which might have been inscribed all over the tabernacle, are *'Christ is all, and in all.'* "

If these sermons prove the means of leading one soul to Christ, who knew Him not before; or of causing any who have known him to have a fuller and deeper sense of His unspeakable preciousness, I shall feel abundantly recompensed for the labor bestowed upon them. To know Him as the mercy-seat, and to have access to him in that character, is the first and greatest of all possible blessings. Believers in Jesus, this is a matter on which you can speak from experience. You know the privilege of prayer, the joy of communion with Him who "dwelleth between the cherubims." Make full proof of your privilege. A spring of water cannot well be hid. It will gush out and flow along, spreading verdure and beauty wherever it goes. Every Christian should be a spiritual spring, a fountain of blessing in the circle amidst which he is placed. A ray of light cannot be hid. It is made to shine. It must shine. And as it shines, it gilds and brightens some object or other on which its radiance rests. But every Christian should be a ray of light,—a spiritual sunbeam. Hence the apostle exhorts Christians to "shine as lights in the world." Yes, and those who know the mercy-seat, and the blessedness of access to it should be sunbeams indeed, examples, wherever they go, of peace and cheerfulness, serenity and joy. The Psalmist speaks of it as the duty of those who know God, to be—in the highest and noblest sense of the good old Saxon word—"*merry* and joyful." If we have access to the mercy-seat, and enjoy its privileges, let us strive so to live that our whole spirit and bearing shall testify to those about us that religion is to us an element of gladness, and that we are abundantly satisfied with the plenteousness of God's house—even of his holy temple.

One thought for those who are not Christians. The tabernacle, with its services,

THE MERCY-SEAT. 393

was designed for the salvation of men. But, if every part of its heaven-devised arrangement was intended, in the way of illustration, to represent Christ, then, it is plain, that in the matter of the soul's salvation *Christ must be everything*. To be without Christ is to be without all that is essential. If you have Christ you have everything, if you are without Christ you have nothing. No language can properly express the spiritual poverty of those who have no part in Christ. They have no pardon, no peace, no strength, no righteousness, no portion for eternity. Beloved hearers, out of Christ *this* is your condition. Will you remain in it? Oh, seek Jesus on the mercy-seat. He will bless you—and then you will be blessed!